JFL Judson Family Life Series
Jan and Myron Chartier, general editors

The Springtime of Love and Marriage

Guidance for the Early Years of Marriage

James R. Hine

Judson Press ® Valley Forge

Other books in the Judson Family Life Series

Help for Remarried Couples and Families
Caught in the Middle: Children of Divorce
Letters to a Retired Couple: Marriage in the Later Years
Live and Learn with Your Teenager
Child Rearing in Today's Christian Family
The Church in the Life of the Black Family

THE SPRINGTIME OF LOVE AND MARRIAGE

Copyright © 1985
Judson Press, Valley Forge, PA 19482-0851   9/91

Bible quotations in this volume are from the Revised Standard Version of the Bible copyrighted 1946, 1952 © 1971, 1973 by the Division of Christian Education of the National Council of the Churches of Christ in the U.S.A., and used by permission.

Library of Congress Cataloging-in-Publication Data

Hine, James R.
  The springtime of love and marriage.

  (Judson family life series)
  Bibliography: p.
  1. Marriage—United States.   2. Courtship—
United States.   3. Family—United States.
4. Communication in marriage.   I. Title.   II. Series.
HQ734.H632   1985   646.7'8   85-14664
ISBN 0-8170-1064-5

The Seasons of Love

To love in the spring
Is to feel the heart sing.
New love is fresh,
Expectant, mysterious.
It is emotion's new flame
To be guarded and nurtured.

Love in the summer
Is hot, intimate, compelling,
Leaping between
Calm and storm,
Never boring,
Always exciting.

Love in the fall
Is mellow.
Autumn colors are warm—
Stimulating reds and yellows,
Inviting walks in the woods
And intimacy.

Love in the winter
Is warmed by the glow of
A crackling wood-fire,
Before which we hold hands
Remembering the past,
And dreaming of the future,
Feeling comfortable and secure.

Enjoy the seasons of love
As they come and go.

—James R. Hine. 1984

Contents

Editors' Foreword

James R. Hine has been contributing to the health of marriages for most of his professional life. He has provided a number of published resources to this end. In writing *The Springtime of Love and Marriage* he has made another important contribution to the volume of literature on marriage.

His book is the fourth in a series of books being published by Judson Press on marriage and family for contemporary Christians. The purposes of the Judson Family Life Series are to inform, educate, and enrich Christian persons and inspire them

    a. to become acquainted with the complex dynamics of marriage and family living;

    b. to pinpoint those attitudes, behavioral skills, and processes which nurture health and wholeness in relationships rather than sickness and fragmentation;

    c. and to consider marriage and family today in light of the Judeo-Christian faith.

As editors of the Judson Family Life Series, we are committed to making available the latest in family life theory and research and to helping Christian families discover pathways to wholeness in relationships. Every attempt will be made by the authors to apply new insights to the realities of daily living in marriage and the family.

Volumes in the series will focus on the stages of marriage, divorce and remarriage, parenting, the black family, and nurturing faith in families. Each will be designed to deal with specific issues in marriage and family living today.

The Springtime of Love and Marriage draws heavily from Jim Hine's experiences as a pastor, campus minister, counselor, and professor. Since 1972 he has been studying what characteristics contribute to well-functioning, long-term marriages. His first thorough treatment of his findings were the subject of his book *What Comes After You Say, "I Love You"?* He uses findings from these studies to guide those contemplating marriage or who are in the early years of their marriages. With these experiences and his research Jim Hine has written a book full of wisdom for those about to be married and newlyweds.

One of the strengths of the book is its solid Christian perspective. Those in the early years of marriage will find here theological reflection and thought that has practical value for their future years together. This is a book about what young married relationships ought to be and can be.

James R. Hine is currently an adjunct professor in the department of child development and family relations at the University of Arizona. He also has a private practice in marital and family therapy.

It is with a real sense of joy that we introduce you to Jim Hine and his book on marriage in the early years.

Jan and Myron Chartier
The Eastern Baptist Theological Seminary
Philadelphia, Pennsylvania

Acknowledgments

Acknowledgments are generally written after a book is finished. It is then that an author realizes the debt he or she owes to the many hundreds (should I say thousands?), who were the "cloud of witnesses" and helpers in the process of putting ideas into words about a particular subject. One is reminded of the Academy Awards ceremonies where a producer, writer, or performer attempts to thank everyone, beginning with father and mother and coming down through all the people who had anything to do with the particular production or person being awarded.

I also would like to include all of the people who had anything to do with my writing this book, even Miss Wood, my strict, demanding high school teacher who first taught me how to discipline myself in the art of writing. Since it is not possible to acknowledge everyone, except in my mind's capacity to recollect, I shall limit myself to thanking all the couples in my study of competent marriages, who walk back and forth across the pages of this book, playing parts to illustrate how people should behave in married life. I am grateful to my wife, Janet, who tolerated all the hours spent away from her and our marriage so that this book could be written. I also thank her for her willingness to read it chapter by chapter as it was produced in order to make corrections and comments. I would not want to omit Jan and Myron Chartier for asking me to write it in the first place and David Mace who has encouraged me in all my efforts to stimulate growth and enrichment in marriages.

I hope I have given credit to others in the field, whose research and writing have helped me. No person is an "island [but] part of the main" when it comes to writing a book, and that certainly goes for me. Thanks to all of you.

James R. Hine

Preface

How can one best study the ingredients of a well-functioning marriage? One might conduct a survey of a large number of sound marriages by asking the couples involved to check a list of attributes they thought had a profound effect on their marital competency. The results would be interesting but only temporarily helpful. Why? Because people change and the way a marriage looks today may be quite different a year from now and certainly ten years from now. It is the difference between a still picture taken at one moment in time and a series of pictures taken over an extended time sequence or motion pictures taken from time to time. With a series of pictures or movies one has the opportunity to observe the change that is taking place, thus getting a better evaluation.

In the early 1970s I decided to begin this kind of longitudinal study of well-functioning marriages to determine if I could define what characteristics supported such marriages over a period of time. I started with nine couples in 1972 and added nine more in 1973. Since then couples have been added until now there are over sixty-five couples in the study. I will use results of this study, when appropriate, to provide material for this book. These couples have given me their opinions about why they thought their marriages would work before deciding to enter them. Also, they have commented on the various problems and decisions they had to make in the first years of their marriages.

The first chapters of this book will explore the period before marriage: how couples meet, get to know each other, develop serious relationships, and prepare for marriage. The rest of the book will address such matters as getting a good start in marriage, developing important skills that will be needed in the marriage, and methods for helping the marriage grow and become richer over the years. It is known that most problems that cause serious difficulties in a marriage arise in the first years of that marriage. This makes it doubly important for a couple to work conscientiously during those years in order to get a good start.

It is hoped that those who buy this book will not only read it but will use the suggestions in it for exercises in self-evaluation and development and for preparing with a partner for the rewarding experience that a healthy, happy marriage can bring.

James R. Hine
Tucson, Arizona
January 11, 1985

Section I
Buds and Blossoms

CHAPTER *1*

Are You Ready for Marriage?

As I finished my second counseling session with Harry and Marybel, I asked myself, *Should these people have married each other in the first place?* According to Harry, they hadn't related to each other well from the very beginning. The answer was, *No, they should never have married each other.* Then a second question came to my mind that might take still more courage to answer: *Should either of them have married anybody?* Now, how could I dare harbor the thought that maybe neither should have married anybody?

Perhaps at this point I should backtrack a bit and say that in my experience as a marital therapist over many years I have seen people, some married and some single, whom I thought would be better off in the single life. There was something about them that seemed to make them unfit for the kind of relationship which makes a marriage function. For example, a young woman called me one day and tearfully explained that after three years her husband wanted out of the marriage. "Does he not love you anymore?" I inquired. "Oh, yes, he still loves me," she said, "but he says he feels trapped in our marriage. He wants to be free to live his life just as he sees fit." Now either he wasn't ready to be married or he is the type of person unsuited for a partnership arrangement. An excessive desire for privacy and freedom makes one unfit for marriage.

Such an excess wasn't Harry's problem. Harry was irritable, full of complaints, and pessimistic. He blamed everyone, including Marybel, for any misfortune he had encountered. In other words, Harry was not the kind of person with whom most people could live. Marybel had a volatile personality—explosive, quick-tempered, argumentative, and rigid in her points of view. One can readily see why they had problems in their attempt to live together. And it is very possible that they would have had problems living with anyone.

I believe one could safely say that people like Harry and Marybel, people who are neurotics, do not fit well into marriage and family relationships. I suppose there is such a thing as a compatible neurotic couple. All of us have seen such a couple once in a great while. They seem to be able to get along with each other even though they can't get along with anyone else. Neurotic characteristics include pessimism, hostility, rigidity, lack of affection, selfishness, excessive anger episodes, resentment, jealousy, depression, and unusually low levels of self-esteem. These traits militate against well-functioning interpersonal relationships.

Now let us look at the positive side. The longitudinal study described in the Preface showed clearly that couples, performing competently and happily in their marriages, had certain individual characteristics that helped in this process. This fact could have been observed before any of these people entered into marriage. We will take a close look at Betty and Bill, one of the couples. What characteristics does Bill see in Betty? On the Personality Inventory he rates her as excelling in dependability, maturity, unselfishness, thoughtfulness, warm-heartedness, organizational and domestic skills, neatness, communication, affection, frugality, articulation, listening skills, and truthfulness. Is she lacking in any of the personal characteristics that are needed in a well-functioning marriage? Bill says, "No."

Now let's see what Betty thinks of Bill. She indicates that he excels in dependability, adaptability, maturity, unselfishness, humor, thoughtfulness, geniality, social skills, emotional maturity, ability to relax, energy, communication, affection, initiative, articulation, listening skills, tolerance, optimism, and courage. Does Betty think Bill is lacking in any characteristics important to marriage? Betty states emphatically, "No." This couple has been married for twenty years. I knew them both when they were dating on a university campus and counseled them before they married. I thought they were excellent prospects for marriage and for each other, and I was right. Each had a high "marriageability quotient." This is something to be observed carefully in oneself and in one's prospective marriage partner before any decision is made to enter a permanent relationship.

At this point it might be well to ask, How does one obtain a high "marriageability quotient"? How do these important characteristics develop? To answer this we need to turn to studies that have been done on personality development. Chess, Thomas, and Birch and later Thomas and Chess[1] gave us valuable information by doing a longitudinal study beginning with newborn infants and following them through a number of years of development. In the middle 1950s, when the project was started, 231 children were involved. More have been added since then. In the study the researchers were able to classify the individual characteristics of an infant's behavior, which are displayed from the beginning in various ways, under nine categories: (1) approach/withdrawal—how did the baby behave when presented with a new experience? (2) intensity of reaction—what was the threshold level of the baby's sensitivity to noises, heat and cold, things he saw and tasted, pleasure and displeasure? (3) quality of mood—how much contentment or discontentment was registered? (4) distractibility—how easily could a person get the baby's attention? (5) persistence and attention span; (6) activity level—how much did the baby move around? (7) rhythmicity—what was the predictability and/or unpredictability in time of any of the baby's functions, such as sleep-wake cycle, hunger, feeding patterns, and elimination schedule? (8) adaptability—how did the baby respond to changed circumstances? and (9) threshold of responsiveness—the intensive level of stimulation that is necessary to evoke a discernible response from the baby.

The conclusion is that we are all born with certain observable characteristics which, for the most part, are variations of these nine categories. This explains, in part, our differences in temperament. These characteristics begin to interact with various environmental factors as soon as we are born; so we change as we grow older, but in some measure always retain some of these original biological characteristics. Some of the changes will be caused by parental nurture or special environmental circumstances. Researchers conclude that these changes will take place as long as a person lives. There is no point in the life of a child or adult in which temperament is "fixed" permanently. The biological and environmental aspects of our lives are wedded together and cannot be separated as some have tried to do.

Let us now return to the questions: Why do we behave the way we do and what are the possibilities for change? How does one obtain a high "marriageability quotient"? I believe Chess, Thomas, and Birch have helped us in several ways. First, their conclusions help us to better understand ourselves and why each one of us is unique. Also, they give us hope for change and improvement. We need not stay the way we are. We need not say, "This is the way I am and I can't do anything about it!" This hope for change is in line with the Judeo-Christian concept of rebirth and renewal through confession, rededication, and life in the Spirit: "But the fruit of the Spirit is love, joy, peace, patience, kindness, goodness, faithfulness, gentleness, self-control; against such there is no law" (Galatians 5:22-23).

Are you ready for marriage? Or if you are already married, are you the best you can be for that state? No one has ever reached his or her potential in this respect, but anyone can move toward it.

I ask the students in my university class to list their strengths and weaknesses that might affect their relationship in a marriage. They are very honest about the matter and make two lists from what they know about themselves. It is good for them to recognize their strengths in order to develop confidence and self-esteem, but what does a person do with his or her weaknesses? Acknowledge them; try to understand them, and get involved in the process of change.

In my longitudinal study of well-functioning marriages I found certain personal characteristics which my subjects revealed in their relationships. I will list them for your use in rating yourself.

Characteristic	Lacking	Possesses to Some Degree	Satisfactory	Excels
1. Dependability				
2. Trustworthiness				
3. Warmth, affection				
4. Ability to give and receive love				
5. Generosity and unselfishness				
6. Ability to meet crises				
7. Mental and emotional maturity				

Characteristic	Lacking	Possesses to Some Degree	Satisfactory	Excels
8. Honesty and openness				
9. Will to succeed in the marriage				
10. Sense of humor				
11. Durability (wears well; does not give up easily)				

Suggested Activity for Chapter 1

1. Check the personality characteristic scale to determine your rating for each item. Note the characteristics on which you are strong and those on which you need to work.
2. If you are engaged or are involved in a serious relationship with someone, ask him or her to use the scale. Compare your results.
3. If you are married, rate yourself and your mate on the scale. Compare your results.
4. Select a couple you believe to have a stable marriage and ask them what personality characteristics they believe to be most important for a good marriage.

CHAPTER 2

The Dating Game

Some years ago I gave a lecture at a women's college in Beirut, Lebanon. In the question and answer period following the lecture, one of the students said, "Tell us about dating in America."

I should not have been surprised at the request, but it took me a moment to prepare myself for an answer. I told them about how young people in my country meet, often informally and without parental help, agree to go out together, and if they like each other enough over a period of time, they may decide personally to become engaged and later be married. It would be putting it mildly to say that they were interested in what I had to say.

After awhile I asked them, "Tell me how you manage to meet and marry here in the Middle East." One of them replied, "We don't date the way your young people do. Our parents arrange our marriages." I asked, "Is anyone here engaged to be married?" A beautiful young woman with black hair and dark flashing eyes held up her hand and said, "Yes, I am engaged." "Tell me about the young man you are about to marry," I asked. "Oh, I have never seen him! I will see him for the first time at the wedding. But my parents have been very kind to me. They have allowed me to see his picture," she replied.

This seemed to be the case with most young people I met throughout Asia. In India I had some lively discussions with college students on this subject. Although they were interested in the dating system as practiced in the United States, most of them thought their way was better. And the argument frequently was, "It must not work so well for you. Just look at your divorce rate as compared to ours." At one of the colleges in northern India where I spent a considerable amount of time, there was very little intermingling of the sexes. In some of the large cities old customs were beginning to break down and a form of dating was practiced. In the villages, however, parents arranged the marriages as has been done for centuries.

Students in my university classes in the United States find it hard to believe that in many societies of the world courtship rituals take place in a highly segregated situation for females. In most cultures young women are not permitted to meet members of the opposite sex until parents approve. (Even in our country, the sexes were segregated socially until the beginning of the twentieth century. The first time a man called on a woman was a sign of his interest in marriage. In our present time the first date usually has little to do with an interest on the part of either person for marriage.) In Eastern cultures, young people and certainly their parents argue that it takes mature judgment in a matter as important as choosing a life partner, and young people do not possess this kind of judgment. As one young woman put it, "I know my parents will choose a very wonderful partner for me whom I can learn to love." In other words, love would come later; it was not an immediate consideration. The important matters were social status, similar family systems, financial arrangements, prospects for the future, and perhaps health and children. With the emergence of dating in our society, the whole matter was turned around. Love came first. The romantic notion prevailed among many: if you love someone enough, then all other matters can be negotiated. This, of course, has not been the case in many instances.

If we take a critical look at the dating system as we know it in our culture, we may be able to use it in a more productive way. We need to ask: "Why has it failed in so many ways, and how can we correct some of its faulty procedures?" The youth in our culture are going to continue to date and use dating as an avenue to marriage. They are not going to accept the systems of other countries and cultures—no matter what the advantages might be. All of us want the freedom to choose our respective mates. Freedom is a very important part of our democratic way of life. Adolescents are in the process of becoming independent of their parents and their elders; therefore, they want the privilege of choosing a partner without interference from them. This has led to what some have called the most hazardous and complicated method of mate selection imaginable: two people in late adolescence or in their early twenties, a time when maturity and wisdom are in their initial stages, make what might be the most important decision they will ever make in their lives. An objective observer might conclude that this choice is made at a time when people are least able to make it.

Research on the relationship of age to marital stability tells us something here. Bumpass and Sweet[1] showed that marriages taking place under age seventeen were almost twice as unstable as marriages taking place between twenty-two and twenty-four. Marriage instability decreased from a factor of 43 percent for those between ages fourteen and seventeen to roughly 2 percent for those over thirty. Every additional year of maturity provides an additional safety factor to the enduring quality of the marriage. Chronological age is not always related to maturity, but it is a fairly reliable indicator.

Immaturity looks at superficial factors at the expense of more important matters. Physical attraction is a prime example. An immature person is often misled by personal appearances. In fact, all of us are misled more or less by this same phenomenon. In a Roper poll taken in 1984 it was discovered that of one thousand men surveyed, the first feature they noticed was a woman's figure and build (45 percent), the second feature was her face (34 percent), and the third feature was how she was dressed (29 percent). Women reported that they first noticed how men dressed. This is natural because we first notice a person's physical appearance; but if we never see beyond the surface, we never see the real person. When we talk about mature love in chapter 5, we shall think about this matter of seeing beyond the physical in greater detail.

Another factor often overlooked is that a person changes rapidly between the ages of sixteen and twenty-two. Perhaps there are greater physical, emotional, and sociological changes during this time than any other time in one's life. Life goals and values are often firmed up at this time. Religious beliefs are reconsidered and reshaped to form life patterns. And it is the last time that one will have a chance to do those things that one wants to do as a single person, such as meeting a wide variety of persons of the opposite sex, traveling to some faraway places, getting started in a vocation that might involve some financial risks, or being totally free for a year or two without responsibilty for another person.

One important way we can help the dating system function is to educate people to delay marriage until they are mature enough to accept this very adult responsibility. There is some evidence that couples currently are marrying a year or two later than couples did formerly. This could be a healthy trend. Young people who postpone marriage until they are sure they are ready are often those who have certain goals and objectives they wish to achieve before marriage. Education is one of these goals and it is a very important one. I have known many college students who have waited to marry until after they received their undergraduate degrees. I have observed that marrying while one or both partners are still undergraduates brings a lot of stress and tension into the life of couples.

One consideration for young people is to think of dating as an effective way to learn about other people, what they are like, what it means to relate to different behavior patterns, how to communicate effectively, and how to arrive at a wise decision about the kind of person that might make a compatible life partner. By dating, males learn more about females, and females learn more about males. Though this chapter is titled "The Dating Game" (because that is a popular phrase), dating should not really be thought of as a "game." Rather, it is a type of process that is important to one's development in becoming skilled in interpersonal relationships.

Unfortunately some young people insist on using dating as a game in which they hope to achieve status, enjoy free entertainment, win sexual privileges, relieve boredom, defy parents, or exploit one another out of selfish motives. A student in one of my classes described dating on the campus as a game in which there was offense versus defense: The males were always on the offensive pressing for sexual favors; the women were on the defensive trying to hold the line. That kind of a game could only end with each side losing.

The Judeo-Christian tradition has emphasized the dignity and worth of the individual. Each person, male or female, is a child of God. Each person deserves respect, understanding, and encouragement. With this in mind, dating could be a very useful way of promoting development and growth and could make way for healthier and happier adults in marriage in particular and in life in general.

As was said earlier, dating is here to stay. It is part and parcel of American culture and will be practiced in some form by our children and our children's children. Therefore, it deserves considerable attention on the part of adults and young people. A question that should get serious consideration is, "How prepared are adolescents for the dating experience?" The answer is: not well enough. Parents, teachers, and church school leaders need to address this question of preparation with serious intelligence. Good books need to be provided for reading. Classes for youth in how interpersonal relationships develop can be helpful. Opportunities for young people to share their questions and problems relating to their experiences with the opposite sex would lead to more intelligent attitudes on dating.

When one person asks another person for a date, each becomes a marriage prospect for the other even though it may be the farthest thing from their minds at the time. The logic of this is that all people who later get married started their relationship on a first date. So the first date is of some importance. When married people are asked how they felt about each other on their first date, all sorts of answers are forthcoming: "I couldn't stand him!" or "I wasn't impressed at the time," or "Well, I guess I thought she was nice." One person remarked, "I ruled him out right away as a marriage prospect." One couple who came in for counseling explained, "We don't know how it happened. One thing led to another and one day we ended up married." None of these people planned at the beginning to marry; yet marriage was the final outcome. Does this tell us we should be selective about people we date? Many young people scoff at the idea. When her parents objected to the man she was dating, Mary retorted, "Well, I don't plan to marry him for goodness sakes!" Maybe she didn't plan to do so, but who knows what might happen.

I have developed an instrument (the Preference Pattern chart) to facilitate an examination of preferences with regard to dating and mate selection. When a person completes the instrument by checking preferences in both columns, it will provoke some new ideas about the importance and purpose of dating.

Preference Patterns for Dating and Mate Selection

The qualities listed here are to be considered and checked to indicate your preferences for someone you would like to date and someone you would like to marry. Use the following ratings: 1 — indispensable; 2 — important; 3 — desirable but not essential; 4 — not a consideration.

Over a period of years, Lloyd Saxton, asked his students at the College of San Mateo in California about qualities they preferred in a date and in a spouse.[2] Males gave in order of preference looks, personality, and sex appeal as the three most valued qualities in a date; for a spouse the qualities were looks, love, and compatibility. Females gave as the top three qualities for a date looks, personality, and thoughtfulness and consideration; for a spouse they were love, honesty, and compatibility. Love does not appear among the qualities valued for a date, as might be expected, but is highly valued in a spouse. Compatibility does not

Your Date					Your Marriage Partner			
1	2	3	4		1	2	3	4
				Physical Attractiveness				
				Pleasing Disposition				
				Good Health and Heredity				
				Educated and Intelligent				
				Ambitious, Industrious				
				Ability to Communicate				
				Friendly and Sociable				
				Responsible and Dependable				
				Kind, Considerate, Thoughtful				
				Similar Religious Background				
				Good Financial Prospect				
				Active in Church or Religious Group				
				Domestic, Enjoys Home Life				
				High Moral Standards				
				Sense of Humor				
				Amusing and Entertaining				
				A quality not mentioned above:				

appear among the first eight qualities for a date, yet it ranks high as a quality desired in a spouse.

Careful consideration of qualities preferred in dates and spouses could lead to a reevaluation of qualities that contribute to healthy relationships of all types, for all of us are greatly influenced and conditioned by the company we keep.

Suggested Activity for Chapter 2

1. Discuss the changes that have evolved in the dating system in the United States since your grandparents' days. What brought about these changes? In your opinion, are the changes good or bad? Why?
2. What are the pros and cons of the arranged marriage as it is practiced in some cultures and of the marriage selection process of dating, courtship, and engagement as practiced in this country?
3. If you are not married, use the instrument to record your preferences for qualities in a date and in a marriage partner and compare the results.
4. If you are already married, use the instrument as a basis for discussing the factors that were important in selecting each other.
5. What is the effect of family background, your friends, and your religious beliefs on your date and marriage partner preferences?

CHAPTER *3*

Strangers in Paradise

On the university campus where I teach there are various stages between dating and marriage. These are not always formally recognized. After two people see one another on a casual basis, they may enter a "going steady" period. If all goes well, this may lead to a preengagement period. If the two partners decide they are reasonably sure of making the relationship a permanent one, they will want to declare an engagement, at which time a ring may be given to symbolize the commitment.

The engagement does not necessarily lead into marriage. I can recall a student coming up to me following the final class session of the term to say, "I want to thank you for what you have done for me. Last night I broke my engagement to the man I expected to marry. As a result of this class I have discovered it would never work." My first reaction was surprise. Then I realized her experience in the class helped her to look at the relationship with her fiancé objectively and realistically.

Joanne reported an opposite type of experience concerning her engagement and its aftermath. One day she asked me if she could have fifteen minutes of class time to tell her story, which she thought might be helpful to others. She had dated Bob for over a year. Then they agreed to become engaged. They had a good time together, mostly going to parties and the movies. As she looked back on this period, she described their experiences together as superficial. They never had any in-depth, serious discussions; they never expressed their deeper feelings to each other.

As the time for the wedding drew near, Joanne began having serious doubts. She shared these with her mother who described them as pre-wedding jitters. Joanne had gone through the usual round of parties and showers that precede most weddings. Invitations had been sent. Elaborate plans had been made for the ceremony and reception. "I simply couldn't walk out on a big production like that," she told herself. So she and Bob married.

"It took about two weeks to convince me I had made a serious mistake," she lamented. "It wasn't long before he told me he had been married before. This came as a surprise and a shock. I soon discovered that he could make no decision of any importance without calling his mother. He was so different from the man I knew in the dating days. I felt as if I had married a stranger." Though Joanne tried to make the marriage work, she and Bob eventually decided on a divorce, having lived together slightly over a year.

The class asked her how something like this could happen in view of the fact she and Bob had dated for over a year. She explained that they never revealed their true selves to each other. "We didn't want to make any waves!" she said. They were strangers in a fool's paradise. How can two people get to know each other well enough before marriage in order to evaluate their chances for success?

A growing phenomenon of the last two decades is a new phase of dating and courtship known as "living together," or cohabitation. Someone has termed it "practicing marriage without a license." In the United States the annual survey of "Marital Status and Living Arrangements" now obtains information on unmarried couples living together. The survey shows that the number of such couples rose 9 percent per year between 1970 and 1977. Between 1977 and 1980 the number rose by 18 percent per year. The proportion of consensual unions among all unions was 1.1 percent in 1970 and 3.1 percent in 1980. If this continues to rise at this same rate, it could amount to a considerable proportion of the population of couples living together in some sort of union.

What is the nature of this trend, and what does it mean for the institution of marriage? What does it have to say about couples trying to get to know each other more thoroughly before marriage? Young people are curious about these questions and are seeking help from the church, the classroom, and their peers.

Marriage and cohabitation are two different worlds. Many young people came out of a cohabitation relationship hurt, disillusioned, resentful, with a loss of self-esteem, and a lack of confidence in ever being able to sustain a permanent relationship. One young woman, who had been very much in love with her live-in partner and hopeful of marrying him, reported to me that he had just told her he was tired of the arrangement and was moving out. She was devastated. Perhaps it is those who break up who suffer most. One rarely hears from the live-in couples who go on to marry satisfactorily.

In one study, problems reported by twenty-nine upper class female students who had experienced thirty-five cohabitation relationships were mostly in the areas of overinvolvement (loss of identity, lack of opportunity to participate in other activities or with friends, overdependency), jealousy of partner's involvement in other activities or relationships, feeling of being trapped, feeling of being used, and guilt.[1] Judging from my experience with cohabitating couples who have come to me for counseling, I would say these are common problems in many instances. One might add that these same problems are seen in the early years of some marriages.

One of my concerns about cohabitation and the amount of premarital sexual activity practiced by many couples today is the effect all of this will have on the significance of the institution of marriage itself. Is marriage being weakened? Is it losing its "sacramental" nature? Will it be difficult to define marriage as a distinct and separate state from other forms of intimate relationships? Robert Blood states it this way: "If couples engage in sexual intercourse or begin living together before the wedding, they will be half-married already. For them the boundary line between not being married and being married will be blurred."[2] When I was married many years ago, I felt it was an awesome, wonderfully new, and different experience. In retrospect I believe it was good to feel that way about it.

What does the Judeo-Christian faith have to offer in the way of wisdom and guidance? In the Old Testament we find many different kinds of heterosexual relationships: polygyny (one husband, more than one wife); the possession of concubines (secondary partners—not wives—who bore children); and monogamy (one husband, one wife). Divorce was permitted; adultery was not. In the New Testament Jesus gave us a fundamental principle by which we may evaluate all laws and practices related to a marriage (Matthew 19:1-8). The principle came as a result of a question put to him by the Pharisees. They were trying to test him by forcing him to respond to an ancient law applying to the breakup of a marriage. They asked, "Is it lawful for a man to divorce his wife?" Jesus replied by asking them a question: "What did Moses command you?" They answered, "Moses allowed a man to write a certificate of divorce and put her away." Jesus responded by making a distinction between a law (a rule established by a particular society) and the order of creation (God's purpose for the human race): "For your hardness of heart he wrote you this commandment. But from the beginning of creation, God made them male and female. For this reason a man shall leave his father and mother and be joined to his wife, and the two shall become one. So they are no longer two but one. What therefore God has joined together, let not man put asunder."

Here the marriage relationship is put into a theological and spiritual dimension. The passage tells us something about the difference between the mores of a society and the divine plan for the human family. It says something about the nature and significance of a person. It says something about the marriage bond as being sacred, permanent, and good for human welfare. It says something about the meaning of life itself. Know this and then make your decisions and value judgments about human relationships, sexuality, love, and commitment. It tells us that we must take the process leading to marriage in a profoundly serious manner.

Consider, then, the fact that the decision to marry, the choice of a marital partner, and the process leading to marriage could be the most important transactions in one's life. The future of the institution of marriage and the family depends on how we respond to these transactions. Therefore, it behooves one to work through them with all the intelligence and prayerful preparation possible. What can one do, and will it make a difference?

There is something to be said about the time frame itself. It takes time to know another person well enough to make a decision about marriage, so patience is needed. I discovered that the couples in my study did take ample time to know each other before deciding to marry. Most of them went through the traditional stages of dating, courtship, serious involvement, and engagement. Such a journey is helpful because it indicates a gradual development in the relationship over a period of time. Impulsive people are apt to skip over these important developmental stages and make hurried and often unwise decisions.

In looking back over the twenty-eight happy years of her marriage to Norm, Doris, one of the wives in our longitudinal study of couples, comments: "Before getting married, we'd known each other for five years and were still friends." That says a lot, doesn't it? And if a couple who takes two years or more between the first date and the wedding also participates in a marriage preparation program, this is additional insurance for a healthy, well-functioning marriage. If all couples would follow this pattern, I predict the divorce rate would decrease at least 50 percent.

Graduate students in my "Methods in Marital and Family Therapy" classes, as an assignment, work with engaged couples who desire to experience a premarital training program. The results achieved over the past five years have been most reassuring. Each couple writes an evaluation of their experience in the program. The students use a manual which I prepared to guide the couple through the process.[3]

Seven sessions are suggested, six before the wedding and one some months after the wedding. The subjects to be considered in the sessions are as follows: What You Bring to Marriage; Adventure into Mutuality; Personality Traits Compared; The Marriage Union, Emotional and Sexual Characteristics; Financing the Home and the Future; and Religion and Marriage. The final session is designed to be with the clergyperson or counselor in the home of the couple several months after the wedding.

The title of this chapter is "Strangers in Paradise." This is the way all lovers begin their relationship, I suppose. They are in a state of euphoria. In reality, however, they are still strangers groping to understand the meaning of this paradise they have found together and eagerly trying to know each other more thoroughly. It is hoped that given enough time, the strangers will become good friends with a greater knowledge of themselves and each other, convinced of the possibilities that lie ahead for the marriage and dedicated to making those possibilities into realities. Like a flowering plant, love in the springtime is fresh, beautiful, fragile, and desirous of growth into maturity. It needs sunshine, nourishment, and tender loving care.

I offer twelve suggestions as a way to summarize some of the steps a couple might consider as they progress through the various stages and rituals of dating, courtship, and engagement.

1. Endeavor to know yourself as thoroughly as possible. Take a personal inventory of strengths, weaknesses, etc.
2. Attempt to know the other person as completely as possible. Be honest and open, revealing your true self to the other person. Don't attempt any cover-up.
3. Visit in each other's homes. Compare your family backgrounds. What are your concepts of marriage and home life?
4. Review your interpersonal experiences thus far in your dating and courtship experience. Are you temperamentally compatible?
5. Discuss the degree to which you share similar religious beliefs and practices, values, goals, and concepts about roles in marriage and family life.

6. Do you have healthy sexual attitudes and practices? Are you free from negative feelings about sex? Do you anticipate an active and joyful sex life in your coming marriage? Read a good book on sexuality together.
7. Do you both like and want children? How many? Discuss your views on child rearing and development.
8. What income do you need as you begin your married life? Discuss budgeting and money management.
9. Discuss how you both think love has developed and grown since you first began to date. How will you keep it alive and healthy through your married years?
10. Review your progress in your communications with each other. Recall times when you were confronted with differences of opinion. How can you improve your negotiating skills and your ability to manage conflict and anger?
11. Read together at least one good book on marriage and family life.[4]
12. Ask your clergyperson or marriage counselor to guide you through a premarital education and training program.

Suggested Activity for Chapter 3

1. Write down a record of the early "crushes" you had on other people during the early stages of your life. What did you learn from them?
2. If you are not married, trace the progress of each dating relationship you have experienced so far in your life. What first attracted you to the person in each case? How serious did the relationship become? At what point did a breakup occur? In what way was each relationship a learning experience?
3. If you are currently involved in a serious relationship with another and are thinking marriage might be a possibility, use the twelve suggestions at the end of this chapter as a guide to understanding and evaluating your progress.
4. If you are married, use the twelve suggestions as a springboard for discussing how well prepared you were as you entered marriage. You may want to set some goals for what you need to do now.

CHAPTER *4*

Grounds for Marriage

Many people ask the question, "Can success or failure in a marriage be predicted before a couple enters into it?" I wouldn't want to say that it could, but given a couple willing to work, enough time, and enough information, a person experienced in this area can come close to a prediction.

I had such an opportunity several years ago. I was conducting a seminar on preparing for marriage, and at the closing session I asked for volunteers who would be willing to continue through an intensive program of work on their relationships. Four couples expressed their desire to do so. At the start, two of the couples revealed serious problems relating to differences in religious faith. (Later, we discovered additional problems in one of these couples.) The third couple had dated for a long time but couldn't decide whether to marry, continue courting, or quit altogether. The fourth couple seemed to have good prospects for a sound wedded life together.

We met frequently as a group throughout the two months remaining in the spring semester, then continued by correspondence during the summer. Through tests, inventories, and discussions in the group sessions, we explored almost every avenue leading into their relationships. Near the end of the program it became fairly obvious to all of us that one of the couples was not going to make it. The couple whose relationship had come to a standstill felt they had made progress and decided to continue their courtship. One of the couples who had an interfaith problem made great progress during the summer and was married the following year. The couple that seemed to have the best prospects at the start (Don and Clarissa) never married—Clarissa decided it wouldn't work and ended the relationship with Don. Several years later, Don wrote me a letter:

> You may remember that you counseled Clarissa and me. Fortunately, we did not get married. I think that through the group counseling sessions you directed, some facts about our personalities emerged that ordinarily would not have been revealed. When we did break up, I needed to turn to someone. I shared my feelings with a few friends and they respected my feelings, but they just didn't understand what I was going through. You may remember that Clarissa and I were cohabitating while we were in the group sessions. I felt no guilt about this situation. Yet, when the relationship ended I felt I needed to ask forgiveness from God. I needed to turn my anger and bitterness over to Him, also. I was very angry that Clarissa wanted to break off the relationship. After confessing my burdens to the Lord, I truly felt peace of heart.

Currently Don seems to be doing well and making a good adjustment toward establishing new relationships.

So in three of the four cases we came to what seems now to be the right decisions in light of the realities of each situation. I have not heard how the fourth couple fared. I hope their final decision was a sound one.

If a couple is to seek sufficient evidence to indicate whether a marriage will succeed or not, they must take time, be willing to work, and seek outside resources to supplement what they can do alone. Of course, a couple can never be absolutely sure of a successful marriage, but there are positive indicators that need to be present if they are to work towards it with confidence. When I began my longitudinal study with those first nine couples in 1972 and continued with all the additional couples who have joined the study since, I wanted to find out more about the positive indicators that are important to a well-functioning marriage. I also wanted to know what evidence these couples had in advance of their marriages that convinced them that they were taking the right step. One of the questionnaires filled out by all couples included such a question: "Can you recall what evidence you had before you decided to marry that convinced you your marriage would be successful?" Here are some of the replies.

Mary and Joe have been happily married for thirty-six years. Mary says:

> It never occurred to me that it wouldn't be successful. We'd spent five years of everyday contact in all kinds of circumstances and enjoyed every bit of it. We worked together and played together and did all the big things kids do (if you call 18 to 23 for me, and 20 to 25 for Joe being kids). Having coffee together on the campus was as treasured a date as the most elegant big name band dance— maybe more so. We took marriage courses, continued to read marriage materials, set goals for education and work experience, and completed them before marriage. We found magic in a jillion ways and still do. Perhaps the title of a book, *Make It an Adventure*, summarizes our attitude toward marriage and everything else in life. It really would be hard to fail on that basis, wouldn't it?

Joe comments: "Through an extended courtship there developed an effort to make everything work. We had no problems as to family background, religion, or basic values."

For thirty-six years I have received an annual report from Mary and Joe. Several years ago they visited us in Tucson. They still act like newlyweds. They are the eternal romantics, a model for all couples trying to find out what married life can be. A graduate student made a special study of Mary and Joe along with fourteen other couples in my marriage study. They made a perfect score on the Locke-Wallace Marital Adjustment Inventory.

Norm and Doris live on a Midwest farm. They have been married twenty-eight years. They met at their campus church choir rehearsal. They entered my marriage study program in 1972. I have observed their marriage for twelve years and they have an excellent one. In reminiscing about how he felt secure about their marriage prospects, Norm writes:

> We had similar backgrounds; our environment, parental influences, and education were similar. We both believed that marriage was to be permanent. We shared common interests and goals. We were completely compatible in religious beliefs and practices. There was a sense of completeness when we were with each other and that of incompleteness when we were apart.

Doris adds:

> We had visited in each other's homes a lot and knew what to expect in family traditions—even what both of us liked to eat. We were

old enough to believe this was not a passing fancy (22 and 24), and had known each other for a long time.

John and Jerry met in high school and their parents thought they were too young when they decided to marry. Jerry was 18 and John was 20, just having finished his sophomore year in college. After dating for three years, these two married at an age younger than any other couple in our study. They had five counseling sessions with their minister before marriage. John had completed two years of work toward an engineering degree. After being married, Jerry worked to support John and herself while he finished his degree and obtained work. After having two children, Jerry went back to college and eventually obtained her master's degree in child development and family relations. They became quite active in a church and Jerry says this became a unifying factor that helped the marriage to succeed. Also, Jerry's opportunity to complete her education contributed much to her feeling of fulfillment and her satisfaction with marriage. Even though they were quite young at the time they were married, both felt they had evidence it would function well. John comments:

> We both went into it with absolutely no thought that it could possibly fail. We both tend to believe that almost anything is possible as long as one sets his mind to it; so I don't think we ever thought of the negatives. One evidence for our coming successful marriage was probably friends and relatives who said it would never last because we were too young—so we had to show them!

Jerry explains her evidence this way:

> I was convinced that John was the man for me and the kind of father I wanted for our children. I was willing to give all my energies to being a good wife to a man who was honest, had a good sense of humor, integrity, and ambition. He always made me feel good.

Jerry and John, in spite of marrying so young, turned out to be one of the best marriages I have studied. The early years were not without problems due to being in school, little money, Jerry's unfinished education, and two little children to care for. However, determination, a good sense of humor, deep respect and caring for each other, and a strong religious faith carried them through. After twenty-five years of happiness together John became ill and eventually died, losing a battle with cancer. On a recent visit with Jerry, she shared with me the courage and faith which has sustained her through this traumatic period of her life. She is dating again but can find no man that comes near to measuring up to John.

At this juncture let us turn to some of the results obtained from the couples in my longitudinal study which indicate the necessary ingredients of a well-functioning marriage. If these are used by a couple contemplating marriage, they will serve as a guide to what needs to be taken into consideration as adequate "grounds" for their marriage.

I wanted to know in what areas these well-functioning marriages excelled and what they all shared in common. The results show there were eight characteristics in which all couples were fully functioning. They are as follows:[1]

1. All couples are truthful and open. This is an important factor in communication. Feelings are shared, not repressed. Problems are discussed freely and rationally. Couples admitted communication, in general, was not easy for them, but they work constantly to improve it.

2. They hold a deep respect for each other. As we shall see later, respect is a very important component of love. As you noted in Jerry's profound admiration for John, respect was a clue as to why their marriage was so satisfying. You need to be able to say to your mate, "I'm proud of you."

3. They are mutually affectionate. This demonstration of affection keeps the glow in the relationship. Touching and saying loving words to each other increases confidence and self-esteem and is a constant source of encouragement. It is nourishment for healthy growth.

4. They support and reinforce each other. Each attempts to discover the other's needs in order to meet them. The beauty of reciprocity is that there is no feeling of, "I'm doing more than he is." Or, "She doesn't seem to appreciate how much I do for her." I have called this important process the G.R.P.R. Principle: Gradual, Reciprocal, Positive Reinforcement. No marriage can function without it.

5. They share value systems. The values were often generated by their religious beliefs and their activity in their churches. Almost all the couples expressed their appreciation for the contribution their faith and their churches made to their marriages.

6. They are moving toward similar goals. It is my firm conviction that beliefs generate values, and values determine goals. It is understandable then that these couples should find compatibility in what they want to accomplish in their lifetime together. Similar goals tend to bring the couple closer together with the passing of time.

7. They are meeting the crises in their lives successfully. This illustrates what I have come to believe is an indispensible quality in anyone's life—"coping power." When faced with illness, accident, sudden

change of plans, and so on, these couples do not lose their capacity to function. In fact, they face the situation realistically and decide how to take the first step toward a solution to the problem.

8. They display a high degree of loyalty and faithfulness. This is due to behavior and performance on the part of each that engenders faith and confidence. They are responsible, dependable, dedicated, and always present when needed. This built a foundation of trust without which no marriage can erect a superstructure.

The general conclusions of the study lead me to conclude that a well-functioning marriage must satisfy conditions in four major categories: (1) personal characteristics of individuals; (2) factors that lead to compatibility in the marriage; (3) basic skills and capacity for achieving goals; and (4) favorable situation and environmental conditions. I have attempted in the following layout of these categories and their subdivisons to create an instrument for people to use to determine their grounds for marriage. The format proposes questions which may be answered and evaluated.

Grounds for Marriage

Use the following numbers to indicate your rating in each column: 1. Very much so. 2. Better than average. 3. Satisfactory. 4. Slightly below average. 5. Unsatisfactory, needs attention.

I. *Your Personal Characteristics*

	Male	Female
1. Are you dependable and trustworthy?	___	___
2. Are you warm and affectionate?	___	___
3. Are you generous and unselfish?	___	___
4. Can you meet crises effectively?	___	___
5. Are you mentally and emotionally mature?	___	___
6. Are you durable (long-lasting)?	___	___

7. Do you have the will to succeed? ____ ____

8. Are you honest and open in
   communication? ____ ____

II. *Compatibility Factors*
   1. Do you really like your partner? ____ ____

   2. Do your personalities interrelate well? ____ ____

   3. Do you have many interests in common? ____ ____

   4. Do you agree on marital role concepts? ____ ____

   5. Do you share religious beliefs and
      activities? ____ ____

   6. Do you share common values and goals? ____ ____

III. *Marriage Skills and Capacity to Achieve*
   1. Do you communicate with each other well? ____ ____

   2. Can you negotiate a difference
      satisfactorily? ____ ____

   3. Are you able to meet each other's needs? ____ ____

   4. Do you have adequate parenting skills? ____ ____

   5. Will you perform well together sexually? ____ ____

6. Do you have domestic skills (cook, clean, etc.)? ___ ___

7. Are you skillful at money management? ___ ___

8. Will you attain your vocational goals? ___ ___

9. Will you be satisfied with your proposed income? ___ ___

IV. *Situational Factors*
1. Was your home life a happy one? ___ ___

2. Was your childhood a happy one? ___ ___

3. Do you consider yourself well educated? ___ ___

4. Have you completed most of your education? ___ ___

5. Is your income level satisfactory? ___ ___

6. Will you be satisfied with your geographical location (climate, people, region, etc.)? ___ ___

7. Will you be satisfied with your housing arrangement? ___ ___

8. Will you enjoy having children in your home? ___ ___

9. Do you have relatives and friends who will be supportive and companionable? ___ ___

10. Will you get along with your in-laws?   ___   ___

11. Do you consider yourself to be physically
    healthy?   ___   ___

12. Do you have adequate health and life
    insurance?   ___   ___

13. Are prospects good for few major medical
    or dental bills in the near future?   ___   ___

14. Are you satisfied with your current line of
    work (job, vocation, career)?   ___   ___

15. Do the two of you agree on having pets in
    your home (dogs, cats, birds, etc.)?   ___   ___

When you have finished, compare your results and evaluate your similarities and differences.

Suggested Activity for Chapter 4

1. Would Don and Clarissa have married if they had not had the benefit of the premarital sessions? What is accomplished in such sessions that might be missing without them?
2. Review the evidence given by the three happily married couples that made them sure their coming marriages would function well. List the various factors they mentioned.
3. After rating yourselves in the "Grounds for Marriage" outline, list your strengths and weaknesses. What would you like to do about areas you rated as "slightly below average," or "unsatisfactory?"

CHAPTER *5*

Love: Broad Shoulders?
Pretty Face?

 "I knew the minute I saw her that she was the one for me." I have heard this said many times. What does it mean? Debbie was swept off her feet when she first met Tom. "He was one gorgeous big hunk of man! I adored him from the very start. It was love at first sight." Is it possible to love someone from the very start? Or is this just a romantic fantasy?

I have an experiment which I use in my classes once in a while. I have a series of numbered pictures of men and women. I ask the students in the class to choose the picture of the opposite sex that they would be most likely to marry. I never yet have had anyone say that he or she would not make a choice. They do so eagerly. When I ask them to explain why they picked out a certain one, they reply in terms something like, "That's the one that has the qualities that I like." Apparently most people are quite impressed with the visual image of the people they meet.

A team of researchers attempted to find out what caused college students to want to continue seeing members of the opposite sex after their first meeting.[1] The only factor they could discover was physical attractiveness. Common interests, intelligence, and other qualities might come later, but not at first. There did not seem to be much difference between the men and the women in this case. Other studies show that personal appearance also has a pronounced effect on choosing a person to marry. Why does this happen?

We are conditioned from early childhood to assume personal characteristics from what we see in a visual image. In the first place we learn to think of certain things as beautiful and others as ugly. We know this because what we term beautiful may not be considered so in other cultures. In Western countries slender women are desirable. In certain Eastern countries large women are considered more attractive. Changes occur within a region over a period of time. In my dating days, tall women were avoided. Today tall women are considered very attractive and desirable. Most models today must be tall.

Young people read magazines and see the ads depicting what an agency or manufacturer wants to use to enhance the particular product it is selling. Persons will see the image of a man or woman that is supposed to represent the ideal. And the viewer will come to think of it as desirable. Young people will go to see a motion picture, and here again will be the "stars" that say to the viewers what is considered to be the ideal. After having experienced this repeatedly, the young men or women look over their classmates at school and judge them according to the standards set by the media. They will attempt to choose their dates as closely in tune to these standards as possible.

In each person there is imprinted an image that is considered ideal, and when it comes to loving someone, that image will have a profound effect on the intensity of that love, at least at the beginning. John Money discusses this phenomenon using the analogy of the Rorschach inkblot, where a person is asked to look at the blot and tell what comes to mind. In Money's case the one loved at first sight might be called a Rorschach love blot. A man sees a woman (or vice versa) and suddenly all the imprinting from the past comes into focus and says to the person, "This is what you have been waiting for."[2] I call it the "across the crowded room complex," from a song in the musical *South Pacific*. One person at a party looks across a room at all the people crowded around the refreshment table, sees a face, and something clicks. A wondrous happening takes place. Is it love? Not really, but the visual effect is overwhelming.

I am not trying to put down anyone who is trying to look pretty or handsome. I prefer someone who is neat, clean, dressed in good taste, and knows how to smile. I have no objection to the "seventh heaven" condition in which young lovers seem to be. However, I would like to expose the myth that this is the way it is always going to be and that infatuation is real, genuine love. George Bernard Shaw is given credit for having said on one occasion, "When two people are under the influence of the most violent, most insane, most delusive, and most transient of passions, they are required to swear solemnly they will remain in that excited, abnormal, and exhausting condition continually until death do them part." Let us say to any couple who is under the influence of this "most delusive and most transient of passions" that they had better understand what it is and take the time to work out something more permanent before deciding to marry.

Now we come to the important question: what is genuine, mature love? Is it something to which we must come by passing through a series of stages or phases that might lead us to a place where we can say, "This, truly, is love"? What is this process? In one sense, these phases may be experimental in nature. Just as a child might experiment with many ways of relating to others in developing into an adult, so might the young lover experiment with many ways of dealing with a relationship with the opposite sex. It is hoped that out of this experimental process there might come a healthy, mature form of love.

How can we come to a better understanding of the nature of true love? It is true that we use the word "love" to carry more weight than any one word in a language can possibly carry. We say that we love to go to the movies; we love apple pie; we love our pets; we love people; we love God. Can all of this be love?

The Greeks had a more adequate way of dealing with this concept through the use of three words: *philia*, *eros*, and *agape*. *Philia* was used to denote the relationship between one family member and another. From it we derive our word "filial." It is sometimes defined as the love of friends. *Eros*, from which we derive our word "erotic," is sometimes thought of as sexual love, but I would not limit the word simply to that meaning. Eros, according to Greek mythology, created life on the earth. "Before, all was silent, bare, and motionless. Now all was life, joy, and motion," says an early Greek myth. So I like to think of it as a life-giving force, a social/sexual bonding between two people. The best discussion of this aspect of love is contained in *Love and Will* by Rollo May in which he describes eros as that which "seeks union with the other person in delight and passion, and the procreating of new dimensions of experience which broaden and deepen the being of both persons.[3] *Agape* is a word that is frequently used in the New Testament. In its highest sense it is the love of God for God's children. It is a giving, unselfish love. It can love the unloving and the unlovable. We will examine it more closely later as it is used in 1 Corinthians 13.

Do all of these meanings of love have anything in common? I think so, but I am not sure that I can describe it. To love in the best sense of that word is to relate to that which is important, valuable, dependable, reinforcing, and consistently meaningful. It is something without which life would be less satisfying and worthwhile. It begins and grows according to a principle which I called the G.R.P.R. Principle: It is *gradual* over a period of time; it is *reciprocal* in that it must be a two-way street; it is *positive* in that it must be productive in meeting real needs; and it is *reinforcing* in that one is encouraged and supported in the process of growing. It may differ in terms of a variety of reinforcements. The love of parent, brother, sister, friend, or spouse are not the same, yet all have something in common.

This also raises another question: Can a person like a person without loving that person? I believe the answer is yes. Zick Rubin devotes an entire book to a discussion of this question.[4] I can know a person and admire, respect, and enjoy that person without loving him or her. On the other hand, it would be difficult for me to conceive of loving another person without liking him or her; yet I cannot rule this possibility out completely. One might have a sexual desire for another without liking him or her, but that would not be love in its fullest sense.

Might we not conclude, then, that genuine loves of all kinds have some things in common, but that which many people identify as love may not contain these characteristics?

One's capacity to love and one's "lovestyle" are the result of a learning process that begins in infancy. Once a child is born, he or she is entirely on the receiving end of love. What the child gives in terms of smiling, cooing, or cuddling is not offered as an act of love, but only as a response to what it is receiving from the parent. It doesn't take long for the child to learn to do certain things in order to have its needs met. If the child has loving and caring parents, it responds in a way that prepares it for future loving ways. That child's personality forms in a very different way from that of a child who resides in a neglectful or hostile environment. So the capacity to love begins by experiencing the effects of a loving home life.

Later the child learns how to respond to brothers and sisters and the meaning of equality and fair play. Now it is time for the child to learn how to be thoughtful of others and their needs. This results in a give-and-take process. If one is to receive from others, one must learn to give. Later it is hoped that the child will learn to care for and meet the needs of others—regardless of return. It will be caring because caring is good in itself. This is approaching the *agape* stage. Some have argued that there is no such thing as an unselfish love and that there is a satisfaction derived from caring and giving. I would propose that if one loved and cared for another with the expressed purpose of receiving a reward, then that argument might be true. However, if one expresses *agape* not thinking or caring about what will be received from it, then I believe it approaches a state of unselfishness. Whatever results in terms of a "good feeling" within oneself is then only a by-product of the loving act.

For many years I have been observing the kind of love that is the dynamic force in the happy marriages that I have studied. Is there any way of summarizing the component parts of the love of these people for their spouses? I have tried to do this through the following expressions of love.[5]

1. Love involves a fondness, respect, and admiration for another. The characteristics infer a liking for the other person. We might call this kind of love "affection."

2. Love is developing an attachment to a person found to be sexually/socially desirable. Here *eros*, in its larger sense, comes into play. It might be said that we find in this phase a happy combination of *eros* and *philia*. It is a bonding of mental, emotional, physical, and spiritual components of two people that forms a powerful creative force in their lives.

3. Love is a concern for another—a desire to affirm, to help, to serve. This is the caring part. It arises out of the empathic feeling for another. Here *agape* comes into play. It is a desire to meet the needs of one's spouse and to reinforce his or her best efforts to achieve fulfillment.

4. Love is a search for completeness and fulfillment through another person. Many believe that a single individual is by nature a lonely person with a sense of alienation. This may be accentuated in a world that tends to depersonalize and dehumanize all of us. In addition to this, we are born physically and perhaps emotionally incomplete. We need others. In the most intimate relationship of marriage, there is the possibility that in love we may overcome some of this feeling of isolation. Perhaps God ordained this kind of relationship in the "order of creation" to make life more satisfying and enjoyable. We accept this promise knowing that we must respect each other's privacy and never become overdependent or addicted to each other.

5. Love is a decision and a commitment. This needs to be fully understood. It avoids two pitfalls: one which says, "We will give it a try, and see if it works," and the other, "Somehow love will conquer all our problems." In the one case, we have a couple entering marriage while keeping one foot outside the door for a quick getaway if needed.

In the other, we have the romantic notion that there is no hard work in making a marriage succeed; love will do it all. If there is a lack in many of today's marriages it is in the areas of decision and commitment. When one evaluates a relationship to the point of being able to say that it warrants a marriage, then a decision to marry and stay married will provide a successful beginning. The commitment is in the form of a covenant which is a sacred act pledging oneself to the other to be loyal and faithful to the very end of your days together—"Till death do us part." A psychologist friend of mine said in a class session that he has come more and more to believe that love and decisiveness are inseparable. I agree. You will remember some of the happily married couples quoted earlier, saying, "When we got married, we never gave a thought to the possibility that it might not work. We knew we would make it work." With this kind of determination and courage, few marriages would fail.

It is springtime in Arizona, and we have just planted a tree. Planting a tree, particularly in Arizona, is no simple matter. A large hole must be dug. About one foot below the surface one strikes a substance known as caliche. It is almost as hard as concrete and has been formed over many years by mineral deposits. One must bore through this caliche before striking softer material once again. Before the tree is planted most of the material taken out of the hole must be replaced by a better grade of top soil, mulch, and an assortment of fertilizers. A liquid solution is applied that will help the root system of the tree avoid the shock of being transplanted. Then the tree is carefully placed in the ground, watered, and sheltered from the hot Arizona sun. For many days the tree must be cared for to see that it gets all the water that it needs to keep from wilting. In due time more nourishment will be added. Would you say this represents tender loving care?

Love and marriage in the springtime can find an analogy in the planting of this tree. Careful preparation must be made. Good stock must be selected. Everything needs to evolve in the proper order, taking all the time that is necessary. Then one must understand and encourage its daily growth. Springtime is the time for planting and starting the growth process. It is a beautiful time full of hope and expectancy. Make the most of it!

I would like to close this chapter with a review of the beautiful passage in 1 Corinthians 13. No words were ever spoken or written that will say more eloquently what love can be. The following is from the Revised Standard Version.

If I speak in the tongues of men and of angels, but have not love,

I am a noisy gong or a clanging cymbal. And if I have prophectic powers, and understand all mysteries and all knowledge, and if I have all faith, so as to remove mountains, but have not love, I am nothing. If I give away all I have, and if I deliver my body to be burned, but have not love, I gain nothing (1 Corinthians 13:1-3).

This makes love the paramount issue in life. It is the very essence of life. All other matters are secondary. Therefore, it behooves us to give it first place in our lives. Then Paul continues by stating the characteristics of love.

Love is patient and kind; love is not jealous or boastful; it is not arrogant or rude. Love does not insist on its own way; it is not irritable or resentful; it does not rejoice at wrong, but rejoices in the right. Love bears all things, believes all things, hopes all things, endures all things (1 Corinthians 13:4-7).

One needs to think of each of these qualities in the midst of the hurry and bustle of married life when there are many occasions that tempt us to be irritable or impatient. Four qualities make love consistently present in the relationship: bearing, believing, hoping, and enduring. And because of these, "Love never ends." The chapter ends with a reaffirmation of the fact that love is the focal point around which all life turns:

So faith, hope, love abide, these three; but the greatest of these is love (1 Corinthians 13:13).

It is not easy to sum up the intent of this chapter. From it, perhaps, one can learn the greater dimensions of love. From early beginnings, when tiny roots reach out in the soil to take hold, to the growth period, when love matures and becomes beautiful, we see the maturing process and try to emulate it. Love is a combination of many ingredients. I have tried to mention some of them here. Mature love, full-blown love, is the result of a synergistic effect in which many qualities combine to form an *elan vital*, a life force that holds two loved ones together in a bond so strong that "no man can put [them] asunder (Matthew 19:6).

Suggested Activity for Chapter 5

1. What kind of love is appropriate for the following relationships: (1) Love of parent for child? (2) Love of child for parent? (3) Love

of sister for brother? (4) Love for a close friend of the same sex? Of the opposite sex? (5) Love for a spouse?

2. Read again 1 Corinthians 13. Make a list of the different ways love should be expressed according to this chapter.

3. If you are married, trace the development of your love from beginning stages to more mature ones.

CHAPTER *6*

Does a Contract Sound Unromantic?

All couples enter marriage with contracts, whether they realize it or not. Very few of these contracts are ever written. Sometimes they are verbalized by the partners telling each other before marriage what they expect in terms of giving and receiving, privileges and responsibilities, goals, role performances, relationships with in-laws, affectional expressions, and so forth. They are telling each other that this is what they need and this is what they expect to give. Often these expectations are known by each of the two parties but never divulged. Perhaps they think it too bold to discuss these matters before the marriage takes place. Again, contracts may lie buried deep within the unconscious and are thus unexpressed. For the moment they are dormant, but situations arising later in the marriage may bring them to the surface. Then they are activated. I have had people in a counseling session say something like, "I guess I didn't realize until much later that I expected my wife to carry out the trash." Or, "After being married a year, I became conscious of the fact that my husband was not like my father."

Books and articles are beginning to appear recommending that before marriage, couples express their contracts in more definite terms. By using a prepared inventory of expectations, a couple may discuss matters which will help them understand more fully what each wants from the other and expects to give to the marriage. If every person has a contract

51

in mind before marriage, it follows that two people preparing to marry bring two somewhat different contracts to the marriage. These differing contracts must be forged into one contract if the relationship is to be compatible and satisfying.

Many couples, facing serious marital problems, come to a marriage counselor or therapist indicating that they have conflicting expectations of their marriage. One case comes to mind that illustrates how dramatic a conflict can be. The young wife, married four years, had confronted her husband with, "We have been married long enough now; don't you think it is time we started our family?" "What do you mean?" he replied. "I have no desire to have any children at all!" Upon hearing this, she broke down and cried. Her husband explained that since he hadn't mentioned children before marriage, he took it for granted that his wife knew he had no desire for them. It is difficult for people to understand why they had not talked openly about this before marriage, but they had not. When they confronted the marriage counselor, their question was, "What do we do now?" What would you say to such a question? Here is one person who has no desire for children married to a person who thinks that children are a very necessary and important part of a marriage. Two points of view so different should be dealt with before marriage, not afterwards. If a satisfactory compromise cannot be reached at that time, it might be wise to cancel the marriage.

How definite should a couple be in attempting to agree before marriage on a contract satisfactory to both partners? Many professionals working in the field of marriage relationships are recommending that two people contemplating marriage should give considerable time and attention to defining their expectations clearly and openly. Attorney Jerry Sonenblick insists that a contract should be written and signed to prevent future misunderstandings and disagreements. He writes: "To love is to be committed. To express this commitment in writing for a couple's mutual protection, or to provide safeguards in the event the relationship sours, is an expression of care, a way to help each other savor the joys and endure the pangs of life. The last word in up-to-date domesticity is . . . contracts tailored to fit each couple's expectations and purses."[1] This includes the financial and legal matters of a marriage relationship. Attorneys are especially conscious of the problems couples get into after marriage due to a misunderstanding about what was expected of the marriage in the first place. It may seem to many that a written contract is too legalistic for a couple in love to consider. Each might be hesitant to suggest it to the other. It might be easier to engage in such a process if a marriage counselor suggested and supervised it.

Clifford J. Sager, a psychiatrist specializing in marital relationships, recommends that a couple use worksheets to analyze their needs and expectations and that these be outlined in three categories. The following is an attempt to summarize some of Dr. Sager's suggestions:[2]

1. Categories based on expectations such as love, loyalty, lasting quality ("until death do us part"), children, family life, position and status in society, religion, values and goals.
2. Categories based on psychological and biological needs such as degree of independence/dependence, intimacy, submission and domination, physical and personality characteristics desired in a mate, division of labor in household duties and the work place.
3. Categories that are derivative or the externalized foci of other problems such as communication, problem solving, work and recreational lifestyle, in-law relationships, child rearing practices, spending and saving, habits and manners, friends, and so forth. Dr. Sager believes that any couple taking these categories into consideration before marriage will greatly enhance the marital relationship.

Of course, it would be impossible to construct an adequate inventory to cover all the concerns which a couple should consider before the wedding day. Consider the following contract to be an attempt to help a couple look at some of their important expectations as they plan for their future. It is adapted from an inventory in a manual for couples planning a wedding.[3] Married couples may adapt the contract in renegotiating their marriage.

Premarital Contract

Prenuptial agreements expressed by a couple considering their needs and expectations in their coming marriage.

1. LENGTH OF MARRIAGE. Do I mean for this marriage to last until "death do us part"?

Woman:

Man:

2. CHILDREN. Do I want children in this marriage? If so, how many do I think would be ideal?

Woman:

Man:

3. LOVE AND INTIMACY. Do I need frequent assurances that I am loved and cared for? In what ways do I need to have this expressed?

Woman:

Man:

4. SOCIAL RELATIONSHIPS. Do I want a number of friends that we can share together? Do I want an active social life? If so, in what form?

Woman:

Man:

5. POWER AND DECISION MAKING. Will one of us be more dominant in our relationship? Or will we think of ourselves as equal partners? What will be our method of making decisions?

Woman:

Man:

6. FREEDOM AND PRIVACY. How much freedom and privacy will I need? And in what way will I need this freedom? This privacy?

Woman:

Man:

7. ROLE CONCEPTS. In what roles do I expect to take major responsibility in the marriage? (As homemaker, financial provider, parent,

cook, housecleaner, grocery shopper, bill payer, social director, etc.?)

Woman:

Man:

8. PERSONALITY CHARACTERISTICS. What personality characteristics in my mate do I consider to be the most important? What personality characteristics in myself do I want to emphasize?

Woman:

Man:

9. COMMUNICATION. Do I communicate effectively and do I expect to work diligently to improve my communication skills? Do I expect my mate to communicate with me freely and honestly? Will we set aside special times for communication?

Woman:

Man:

10. CONFLICT AND ANGER. Do I expect to have our conflicts resolved in a rational, sensible way? Will I do my best to use and control my anger in a constructive and loving fashion?

Woman:

Man:

11. RECREATIONAL AND LEISURE ACTIVITIES. In what areas do I expect to have special pleasure in doing things together? Doing things separately?

Woman:

Man:

12. SPENDING AND SAVING MONEY. How much income do I think we will need at the beginning of our marriage? Do I expect to manage our finances by using a budget? Do I want a savings and investment plan? Do I want a joint checking account?

Woman:

Man:

13. IN-LAWS. Do I want a close relationship with my parents? Do I want to visit or be visited by my in-laws often? If one should become dependent, how would I expect to handle this problem?

Woman:

Man:

14. CHILD-REARING PRACTICES. What do I believe to be the most important factor in child rearing? How do I think children should be disciplined?

Woman:

Man:

15. RELIGIOUS FAITH AND PRACTICE. Do I want a strong religious faith for myself? Will I want to be affiliated with a religious organization (church, synagogue, etc.)? Do I expect my spouse to share a religious faith with me? If we have children, do I want them to have a religious upbringing?

Woman:

Man:

16. VALUES. In what areas do I propose to participate to satisfy my cultural and aesthetic interests (music, art, literature, crafts, sports, television, movies, other interests)? What important moral and ethical values do I intend to practice and teach to our children?

Woman:

Man:

17. OTHER AREAS NOT MENTIONED ABOVE:

Woman:

Man:

I find the above to be satisfactory to what I consider to be a healthy, happy marriage. I agree to carry out my part of this agreement to the extent of my ability, and I expect my partner to do the same.

Signed:

Woman ....

Man ....

Date ....

Place ....

Witnesses ....

....

What we expect to contribute to life and what we expect to receive from life develop from concepts generated and acquired from early childhood on. They arise out of needs, desires, and dreams that form images in our minds of ideal states in which we will find satisfaction and happiness. For many, marriage and family life represent a setting in which many of these needs, desires, and dreams will be fulfilled. Two people desiring to unite their lives in marriage bring two different sets of expectations in terms of promises and obligations. Some of these are submerged to the extent that the people are not aware of them. They need to be made aware by some device, such as the premarital contract suggested in this chapter. There are other expectations of which the two people are fully aware but may be hesitant to verbalize in each other's presence. Some are motivated to discuss these matters openly and honestly, and this is to their advantage. Still others will write down what they hope to give and what they hope to get, and this may be better still. If a person marries and finds his or her expectations met in the marriage, that person will be content, satisfied, and fulfilled. If expectations are not met, there will be disappointment and disillusionment. Two people who have the courage and the character to discuss their contracts openly and honestly and attempt in one way or another to formulate a single contract agreeable to both will benefit greatly in the first years of marriage. They will also have a guide that will help them experience positive growth together in a satisfying marital partnership.

Does a discussion of contracts in the form of inventories of needs, expectations, and agreements seem unromantic to you? If so, remember the principle of growth. In order to help a young plant grow into a beautiful flowering shrub, some very practical and earthy things must be taken into consideration. There must be a plan to help it develop from where it is to where it needs to go. The gardeners who engage in this process must agree on this plan. In like manner, couples inarching* their lives together in the springtime of love and marriage will grow and thrive on this same kind of carefully planned beginning. Once you have tried it, you will know how important and productive it can be.

Suggested Activity for Chapter 6

1. Use the three categories basic to marriage contracts listed by Clifford Sager to help you outline your needs and expectations for marriage.

---

*A method by which two plants, with independent root systems, are grafted together by joining the branches.

2. You have experienced a variety of religious beliefs, events, and activities in your life thus far. If you are not married, how would the customs, traditions, and values arising from these experiences affect what you might need in your marriage and your marriage partner? If you are married, how have these influenced your relationship?

3. If you are married or about to be married, consider using the premarital contract suggested in this chapter in order to clarify what you and your partner expect to give and receive in your marriage.

CHAPTER 7

Until Death Do
Us Part

Before writing this chapter, I allowed myself to wander far off on a sentimental journey down memory lane. I have in my study a large file of the weddings in which I have participated over the past fifteen years. (I am an ordained minister as well as a college professor.) In this file I have most of the ceremonies used at these weddings. They are somewhat alike, yet each is a little different. And that difference is the result of the thoughtfulness and sincerity invested in these ceremonies by the couples who were united for life by way of their songs, prayers, Scripture, and vows. As I looked at each one, there materialized the bridal party standing before me, nervous but happy. Here was a moment long planned for. The officiating minister sees something beautiful that most others present cannot see—the faces of the bride and groom as they gaze into each other's eyes and take their wedding vows. All the love, hopes, and dreams that were created over the preceding months come into focus in these solemn promises. And there seems to be a heavenly glow on their faces.

The scene changes, new faces appear as I read each ceremony: Robin and Dave, Kathy and Bill, Monica and Paul, Anne and Tom, Lynn and Wayne, Joan and David, Barbara and David, Grace and Mario, Sue and Lorn, Sara and Tom, Janie and Joseph, Bonnie and Bill, Susan and Steve, Jill and Jim, and on and on. As I think of each couple, I remember how seriously they approached this memorable occasion. All wanted premarital counseling, and all wanted to have a part in preparing the ceremony. Many wanted to write their own wedding vows so that their promises would be in their own words. As a result of the contribution of all these people, a basic ceremony has been created which we will look at later.

As I reflect on this series of joyful experiences with all these couples, I know I have learned from them, and I hope they have learned from me. I think of this learning as coming from a crucible in which many lives and many loves have melted together and formed a beautiful and inspiring pattern for all to follow. What I have to offer in this chapter comes from this kind of intermingling and interacting.

Let us begin by asking, "What is a wedding? What does it mean?" Traditionally, the engagement, the wedding, and the honeymoon have been rites of passage for two people who wish to belong together in a very special relationship for the rest of their lives. The engagement is the path leading to the entrance of marriage. The wedding is the door through which the couple passes, pausing there for a moment to take their sacred vows. Then the wedded couple steps into the inner sanctuary of their life together beginning with a passage sometimes known as a honeymoon. The honeymoon and the wedding trip are one and the same for most American couples, though according to folklorists it used to be a period of thirty days in which the new husband kept his bride in hiding from her relatives. And during this month the newlyweds' drink was mead, a fermented beverage of honey and water, hence, "honeymoon." The honeymoon is the beginning of a long road through the years. Beginnings are important. A happy time spent in a special place will never be forgotten. The honeymoon is a period of transition between single and married life. You won't want to make your honeymoon into a sightseeing tour unless both of you are travel addicts. Select a beautiful place—a resort hotel or cabin where there is ample opportunity for privacy, quiet talks, making plans, having fun in hikes, swimming, tennis, and other activities. Your honeymoon need not be expensive. The bride might suggest to the groom that he need not go to a great expense on it in order to make her happy. Some state parks are ideal for honeymoons, and will cost less than famous resorts. The place and nature of the honeymoon should be agreeable to both bride and groom.

For the couples mentioned in this chapter, the wedding was planned to be a special, meaningful experience for them. I worked with them in helping to choose the place, the music, the vows, and the readings to be used in the ceremony. We wanted the event to be more than a social occasion. I emphasize the fact that the wedding must be planned to meet the couple's needs first. They should determine the setting, the nature of the ceremony, the reception, and the people to be invited. Parents should be consulted, of course, but keep in mind that the couple should make the final decisions.

The weddings we planned were to have a deep spiritual significance, recognizing the words in the introduction of the ceremony, "that marriage is ordained of God and is to be regarded as a sacred act, blessed by our Lord Jesus Christ, and to be nurtured and protected for as long as life shall last." Most of the couples wanted a church or chapel wedding, this being the kind of setting that seemed appropriate for a religious service. The reservation for the church should be made well in advance of the date set for the wedding, and customs and traditions of the church should be taken into consideration. Music should be chosen in consultations with your minister and organist.

Some of our couples wanted contemporary songs, such as "We've Only Just Begun," "Sunrise, Sunset," "A Time for Us," and "Peace I Leave With You, My Friends." I have no objection to songs such as these if the music and text are appropriate and well done. Some churches object to any music that isn't traditional, religious, or classical in nature.

For the reading and meditation almost all our couples chose 1 Corinthians 13. Several chose the passage on marriage from *The Prophet* by Kahlil Gibran; Sonnet XLIII by Elizabeth Barrett Browning; Ruth 1:16-17 beginning, "Entreat me not to leave thee . . ."; Matthew 5:1-12, the Beatitudes; and various readings from the Psalms.

There was a desire on the part of these couples to have family and friends present to participate in the service through unison prayers, responsive readings, and hymns. In one wedding the fathers of the bride and groom read Scripture passages. These opportunities take those who are attending the wedding out of the role of spectators and put them into the role of participants joining in worship with the bride and groom. In addition, they receive the chance to pledge their love and loyalty to the couple in a more visible way.

Lynne and Wayne wanted their service printed in an attractive folder to be used by all in attendance. They worked many weeks, with the two ministers who would be joining in the service with them, creating a meaningful service of worship and dedication.

Earlier in the chapter I mentioned that over the years a basic wedding ceremony had evolved, using some of the traditional ceremonies from different denominations and incorporating suggestions made by various brides and grooms. I keep a number of different services, including some of the contemporary ceremonies, for the couple to read.

Let us look at this one example of a ceremony that has gone through an evolutionary process beginning a number of years ago. The introduction is a welcome to all who have gathered for the occasion. The names John and Jane will be used to represent the couple being married.

You have been invited by John and Jane to share in this happy and holy occasion, and to witness the vows which will unite them in marriage. They wanted you here to join with them in this moment of joy and solemnity, that they might sense your support and love for them as they begin a life together. They bring with them their love, their hopes, their dreams, and their personalities, out of which a marriage will be fashioned, strengthened by the love of God, family, and friends. Together we remember that marriage is ordained of God and is to be regarded as a sacred act, blessed by our Lord Jesus Christ, and to be nurtured and protected for as long as life shall last.

Next, a prayer is given by the minister which asks for God's presence in the ceremony and for a special blessing on the bride and groom.

Almighty God, we ask you to be present and favorable to John and Jane, that they may be truly joined as husband and wife in a covenant made before you. As you have brought them together by your providence, sanctify them by your spirit, giving them a life together which will grow through the years into new and greater forms of usefulness, happiness, and fulfillment. Through our Lord Jesus Christ, Amen.

There follows readings from the Scriptures, almost always including 1 Corinthians 13. Other passages from the Bible may be read, followed by other readings selected by the couple. The wedding pledges follow.

John, will you have this woman to be your wife, and will you pledge your troth to her, in all love and honor, in all service and helpfulness, in all faith and tenderness, to live with her, and cherish her, according to the ordinance of God, in the holy bond of marriage? (Answer: *I will.* The same pledge is asked of Jane.)

The minister asks all those present to take a vow to show their support for the couple as they begin their life together. The minister turns to the congregation and says:

We are asking the family and friends present also to take a vow to support this couple in their marriage. Please answer with, "I will." Will all of you witnessing this ceremony promise to love and support John and Jane as they endeavor to build a happy and successful marriage together?

Family and friends answer, *I will.*

At this point in the ceremony, the bride may be given away by her father or by her father and mother, or parents of the bride and groom may present the couple with their blessing. (The bride and groom also could present themselves or each other without the parent[s] "giving the bride [or them] away.") The question asked by the minister at this time might be:

Who gives this woman to be married to this man?

Reply: *I do;* or, *her mother and I do;* or, *we do.*

In ancient times when the father placed his daughter's hand into that of the groom, it signified that she had been in his possession, but he was now putting her into the possession of her husband. This was considered to be the most important part of the ceremony. However, this has changed altogether in modern times. The daughter is not considered to be the property of her father. She, of her own volition, accepts the proposal of marriage and will from now on be equal with her partner. For this reason in some ceremonies, the minister asks a question similar to this:

Do you, their parents, grant them your blessing, pledge them your love and acceptance, and welcome the new relationship you will now have with your children?

The parents may stand and answer: *We do.*

At this point in the ceremony, the bridge and groom join right hands and take their vows.

I, John, take you, Jane, to be my wedded wife. And I do promise and covenant before God and these witnesses to be your loving and faithful husband. In plenty and in want; in joy and in sorrow; in sickness and in health; as long as we both shall live.

The same vow is taken by Jane, beginning with, *I, Jane, take you, John. . . .*

Some couples like to make these vows personal and devote considerable time in writing them. They may want to say them for the first time during the ceremony as a surprise to each other. Gayle and Tom wrote their vows together and this is what they wanted to say:

Today, I give myself to you and ask for your tomorrows. I promise to love you more than anyone else can. I give to you my love, my strength, and my trust. I promise to be with you and to help you when times are good as well as when they are bad, and ask you to share my triumphs and defeats. Our Risen Lord makes it possible for me to venture a lifetime with you and to trust you enough to open my life and myself to you. I give to you my love and my life and ask you to accept me as your husband (wife).

Then comes the ring exchange. Sometimes a single ring is given, but in most cases today, each gives a ring to the other. The minister says:

What do you give to show that you will faithfully fulfill these vows?

Each answers: *A ring.* Then the minister says: *These rings are symbols of the vows taken here. Their circles represent form and wholeness. They mark the beginning of a long journey together filled with wonder, surprises, laughter, tears, sorrow, joy, frustration, and fulfillment. Wear them that you may know and the world may know you are pledged together through all these things in enduring love and commitment.*

The ring blessing:

Bless, O Lord, these rings, that in giving and wearing them, John and Jane may abide in your peace and continue in your favor unto their life's end. Through Jesus Christ our Lord. Amen.

The rings are exchanged and each repeats:

This ring I give you, in token and pledge, of our constant faith and abiding love.

This prayer follows:

Most merciful and gracious God, bestow upon these your servants, John and Jane, the seal of your approval and your benediction, granting unto them grace to fulfill, with pure and steadfast affection, the vow and covenant which they have made before you. Guide them together through the years ahead, in the ways of goodness and joyful living, that loving and serving you with all their hearts, they may be abundantly enriched by your grace and guidance. In Jesus Christ our Lord. Amen.

Then the minister says:

Will all present join with John and Jane in praying the Lord's Prayer.

All pray.

Then the minister makes a declaration of the fact that he, in his twofold capacity, is authorized to state that John and Jane are to be recognized by the whole world as a married couple:

By the authority committed unto me as a minister of Christ's Church, I declare that John and Jane are now husband and wife, according to the ordinance of God, and the law of the State, in the name of the Father, and the Son, and the Holy Spirit, Amen.

The couple joins right hands and the minister puts his hand over their joined hands and says:

Whom therefore God has joined together, let no one put asunder.

The benediction closes the ceremony:

The Lord bless you and keep you; the Lord make his face to shine upon you and be gracious unto you; the Lord lift up his countenance upon you, and give you peace, both now and in the life everlasting. Amen.

When a couple plans a wedding as carefully and conscientiously as those described in this chapter, a number of purposes are accomplished. Two people declare before the world their intention of being bonded together in love and loyalty for the rest of their lives. They comply with the laws of the state which make certain requirements of each couple desiring to marry in terms of age, residence, a blood test (possibly), and a license. They obtain the blessing of God and the church of the denomination they have chosen. And they surround themselves with family and friends who form a community of love and support at the time of the wedding and in the days and years following. With this kind of a start they have a much better chance to fulfill their vows and promises than one which is held in a secular setting with families and friends not present. This is a fact based on research that has been done on the relation between marital success and the place, the nature of the ceremony, the goodwill of parents and family, and the gathered community of friends who surround the couple at the wedding.

A couple would do well to turn to resources to help them make this a meaningful occasion they will remember for the rest of their lives. Publications by Brill, Halpin, and Genné[1]; and Belting and Hine,[2] and others suggested by a church or clergyperson should prove helpful.

Suggested Activity for Chapter 7

1. Discuss a wedding you have attended and evaluate it in terms of its inspirational quality, the degree to which it was carefully planned, and its religious significance. What about the songs and the music used?
2. List the differences you see in a wedding performed in an office of a justice of the peace with just the couple and witnesses present and one carefully planned and held in a church setting where family and friends are gathered.

3. If you are not married, read through the wedding ceremony in this chapter or another one that might be available to you. What would be appropriate for you; what would you like to change? If you plan to be married sometime in the near future, try writing vows that you might like to use in your wedding ceremony.
4. If you are married, think back to your wedding and the vows you took. What was special about it? What would you do differently? What vows are you ready to make to each other today?

Section II
Fruit on the Vine

CHAPTER *8*

First Steps in the Marriage Dance

Salvador Minuchin, a well-known family therapist, often referred to the way people behaved in marital situations as the "family dance." If one observed this behavior, he could see the movement, the cadence, and the peculiarities of the "dance."[1] How does a couple begin their "marriage dance" together?

First, there must be music. The music has the theme that determines the nature of the dance. There is a great deal of difference between the music of Strauss, which indicates a waltzing step, and the complicated, rhythmic beat of the Cuban music that gave rise to the rumba. The same is true in marriage. If two people come with very different music, their steps and movements will be different and they themselves will be uncomfortable and incompatible. For the music contains the theme consisting of the beliefs, the values, the philosophy, and the theology that motivate and direct the steps of the family dance. What is the quality of the music? Is it well composed? Who is the composer? What does it call for in terms of attitudes, character, and behavior? Are both parties bringing the same kind of music and thereby dancing to the same tune? Your first steps in marriage begin according to your answers to these questions.

It is better to dance on a smooth floor than on rough boards or a gravel road. Here one has to consider the logistics of marriage—the setting, the environment, and the climate. We noticed in the testimony of young couples in the early years of their marriages that what to live in and where to live played an important part in the start they achieved. Some were happier on farms or small towns, others in large cities. Some wanted to buy homes, others wanted to rent apartments. The geographical location was often determined by job opportunities. Having to change jobs, which often involved moving to another location, was never easy. I recently received a letter from a couple who lived in one location for almost thirty years until their children had all left home, and now they are moving into a condominium. In the case of my own family, we have moved three times during our married life, and now feel settled permanently in a location where the climate, the opportunities, and the people are very satisfactory for us. A young couple just starting out can't always be choosy, but there are certain matters to be considered and carefully planned together. Will your location be satisfactory to both of you? You will need a house or apartment that will fulfill your basic requirements. The husband's choice of job and whether the wife will work or not need to be considered. Friends and neighbors are important and will help make the way smoother for you. The church and the community will have support systems that will put a good foundation under your feet.

Start off on the right foot. Ed and Sue were married and drove off on their honeymoon. The car broke down in New Mexico. After a delay and a $500 repair bill, they were on their way. They received a speeding ticket in Oklahoma. In Toronto, their northern destination, their car was wrecked by a valet parking attendant. Ed's suit was ruined in New York City and Sue came down with a case of food poisoning in Boston. Their luggage was lost on their flight back to their hometown in Arizona. It is difficult to believe, but this is a true story. (They even have pictures of these calamities.) Most people would not choose to start married life that way. Of course, much of it was bad luck, which could not be avoided. I have seen recently married people get into marital trouble about as quickly as Ed and Sue got into their predicaments. In one case, within forty-eight hours, the bride registered great disappointment in the actions and manners of her new husband so that counseling was required to get the marriage back on track. I have known couples that spent so much money on their honeymoons that they were deprived of funds which were needed to get started when they came back. Some couples get into needless arguments and quarrels in attempting to make all the decisions and solve all the problems that come during the first weeks of marriage. Resolve to start your dance on the right foot. The other steps will come more readily if you do. Try to begin with effective means of communication. Try to understand each other, and plan your steps together.

Who's leading? In dancing, it is customary for a man to lead the woman. I suppose this is a carry-over from the traditions of the past when men were supposed to tell women where to go (i.e., men defined women's role). Times have changed. Writers in the field of marriage and family relations in the 1920s and 1930s began to speak of the egalitarian marriage, where equality would replace the patriarchal system. In the egalitarian system, husbands and wives regard each other with mutual respect and dignity. Discussion precedes decisions, and an attempt is made to serve the best interests of both people. Power struggles in marriage are unproductive and inappropriate; love, understanding, and fair play should prevail. Attempting to push or drag the other leads to discord and dissension. Remember, you are building a partnership. This does not mean that you will not disagree on a division of labor in which one or the other assumes responsibility. Agree on who is to lead, where and when.

Is the dance work or fun? I have seen couples dance as if it were hard work—and maybe it was. I have seen couples make drudgery out of married life. Jokes are made about getting married as giving up the pleasures of life and "settling down" to routine and eventual boredom. Nothing could be farther from the spirit of the marriages in my study project. Someone has said, "In marriage your joys are doubled, and your sorrows are halved." That is the way it can be and should be. Of course, a good sense of humor helps. Make up your mind you are going to enjoy both the work and the play of married life. In chapter 4 we spoke of Mary and Joe and how their long years of marriage have been full of fun, excitement, and romance. They will never grow old individually or as a couple. Of course, it takes planning from the very beginning. You must keep up the spirit and the joyful music in your dance. Have fun! It will keep the sparkle in your relationship.

Keep in step as best you can. Conrad Weiser coined a word for this — "syncrony" — to indicate harmony in the way two people communicate and relate together.[2] Both have caught the rhythm of the dance and move to the music they have chosen as their theme. Come to common agreements through discussion and negotiation. Communicating with and understanding the other person are ways of creating syncrony. Agree to disagree if you must, but always keep the best interests of the other in mind.

Don't step on each other's toes. This hurts! Avoid making disparaging remarks, being harshly critical, using put-downs, and violating each other's dignity. We all struggle to acquire enough self-esteem with which to live and relate well. Never attack the self-esteem of your partner. It will hurt both of you. We hear today a great deal about spouse abuse. Physically attacking, hitting, pushing, slapping, or kicking the other is unthinkable. Remember, however, that there is also such a thing as verbal abuse. It can be emotionally bruising and damaging. What you do and say, do and say in love. We all need encouragement every day we live. Let us encourage one another as we move together in the marriage dance.

Don't hold on too tightly. You can't dance well if you are being confined, smothered, or held too close. Give each other space and privacy on occasion. While we all need the help of our spouses, we should avoid developing or demanding dependency beyond reason. The couples in our study do so much for each other and yet enjoy an independent spirit that is healthy for the couples and the marriage. Let breezes blow between you. Learn to trust and have faith in each other. Let your embrace be firm and loving, but not confining and possessive.

Remember that you are both learners. Neither is an accomplished artist. Consider yourselves amateurs, knowing a few basic steps, but willing to learn more of the intricate ones. A ballerina friend of mine has been practicing since she was six years old. She admits that she still has much to learn. Think of living together as an art and you and your spouse as budding artists who will spend a lifetime learning the art of relating to each other. There is an expression often used by counselors to their clients: "You don't have to be perfect." When your spouse makes a mistake and starts to blame herself or himself, say, "Remember, you don't have to be perfect — we are both learning." A child, in attempting to learn to walk, often falls. The falling is a part of the learning process. In falling, the child learns better how to keep its balance. I saw a card above the desk of one of the staff members of the church I attend which read, "I am not perfect yet, but God is working on it." Some of the first steps of married life are faltering and sometimes stumbling, but remember that you and your spouse are learners and that stumbling is part of the learning process.

Take an occasional intermission. You don't have to dance together all the time. Some couples think, *Now that we are married, we should be together constantly*. Give yourselves some time apart. Don't be afraid to share your partner with his or her friends. You will do many things together, but not all things together. Sometimes wives feel disappointed that husbands spend so much time at their work place. Wives must realize that husbands often are trying to get off to a good start in their vocations and this does demand a lot of time. On the other hand, husbands must guard against being married to their jobs. Wives with careers outside of the home may overextend their time and energies at their work place. The fact is that these wives, unfortunately, are performing most of the homemaking tasks while engaging in their careers. The couple needs to discuss this possible problem carefully. A good relationship with one's spouse and children is more important than any job can be. However, neither needs to be neglected in favor of the other. Intermissions of all sorts can be used to evaluate and enhance a marriage.

Keep growing and improving. There is a classic joke related to this step. A visitor in New York City stops a stranger and asks, "How do I get to Carnegie Hall?" The stranger replies, "Practice, practice, practice!" My ballerina friend has been practicing for twenty-six years. A professional golfer started practicing at the age of eight. And so practicing should be appropriate in a marriage. I have often advised clients to sit down together occasionally and say, "Let's practice communicating for a while." There are communication games that can be played. Start your marriage by having a mutual understanding that you will be working together to improve your communication, your companionship, your love, your marital dance each day of your married life.

In chapter 6, I mentioned the areas that needed special attention, according to the couples interviewed at the very beginning of their marriages. They were communication, deciding on role responsibilities, managing money, saving time to be together, deciding on having children, managing conflict, achieving a sexual adjustment, relating to parents and in-laws, and changing locations. Most of these areas will be discussed more fully later, but I would like to take a closer look at two of them which will not be emphasized later.

One is the matter of parents and in-laws. In my research project with couples in competent marriages, I inquired about the effects of parents on the marriages of their children. The results indicated mixed feelings on the part of the couples about the positive and negative effects on their marriages. Most of them felt that in-laws were a positive force in their marriage and family life.

You may remember Doris and Norm (from chapter 4), who talked about visiting in each other's homes before marriage and liking what they saw. It was during their courtship days that they developed a good relationship with future in-laws. After marriage there was no great adjustment to make. By being in his home before they were married, Doris even learned what food Norm liked to eat. Norm learned more about Doris's likes and dislikes while visiting in her home. Today they live close to both parents, who now have become loving and helpful grandparents. Being close is considered an asset to this "extended family."

In some cases there is a mother-in-law/daughter-in-law problem. The mother of the groom may be apprehensive about "turning over" her son, whom she has cared for all the years up to now, to an inexperienced young woman. Will he be fed properly? Will his clothes be cleaned in the right way? Will he get the loving care he has been receiving from her? If she makes her feelings too obvious, it will bother her daughter-in-law. Some couples decide to put some distance between themselves and their parents for (at least) the early years of their marriage. This may be for the best in their cases. Studies show that most problems occur between the wife and her mother-in-law; the second highest number of problems is between the wife and her sister-in-law.

One couple came for counseling because the husband was irritated by his wife's parents who were constantly showering them with gifts. If the parents saw anything missing in the way of appliances, clothing, or food, they would be quick to supply it. The husband wanted to think he could take care of their household without outside help.

It is true that one marries the whole family of the spouse, no matter how much one may deny that this is going to happen. Everyone comes along in one way or another. Knowing this, the newly married couple needs to discuss openly and honestly how relations with other family members will be handled, for such handling will have a lot to do with the progress of the marriage.

The other area I would like to look at is finances. Folk wisdom will tell you that money is one of the leading causes of marital difficulties. This is not the case, but it can create plenty of problems if not handled prudently. This matter is of special importance in the first years of marriage for several reasons. The need for material things is particularly great at this time because you are starting out with a new residence that may need furnishing. There will be travel and moving expenses. Certain basic appliances will have to be purchased. The shelves of your kitchen cabinet and refrigerator will need to be stocked. Sometimes a car must be purchased. New health, accident, and life insurance policies will be called for. Most couples enter marriage with a meager accumulation of savings and investments. Their income as newlyweds may be the lowest it will ever be. Yet many couples want the conveniences and luxuries their parents had after years of hard work and saving. It has been estimated that 20 percent of the people in this country are living beyond their means,[3] and a large part of this group is under thirty years of age.

There are six stages of financial need for a family of four. The first is that period before the first child arrives. The second is when the first child arrives, when a 33 percent rise in income is needed. The next period is when the second child arrives, when another 33 percent rise in earnings is needed. The amount necessary for the family decreases 33 percent when the first child leaves home; another 33 percent decrease is noted when the second child leaves home. I presume that this means the son or daughter has finished his or her educational career. The fifth stage finds the couple by themselves once again, and the sixth occurs at the death of one of the spouses. About the same income is needed in the first and fifth stages, adjusted for inflation, although the young couple is more likely to be hard pressed to make it than the older couple.

There is only one way that I know of for a couple to meet these stages successfully as they come along. They must start out with a sound financial plan the first month of married life. This plan means a budget which will help them estimate their income and expenditures and balance one with the other. If you are in this situation, purchase a budget account book available at most drug, office supply, or book stores. Keep track of the amount you spend and the amount you earn. Plan ahead what your short-term and long-term expenses appear to be. Many expenses will occur monthly. Others will come periodically, such as insurance payments, taxes, installments on debts, and so forth. Allow for unexpected bills which generally are car repairs, medical and dental bills, and service calls. Don't let these surprise you and wreck your financial plan. Put them in your budget under "extraordinary expenses."

During the early years of marriage it is wise for the couple to plan for a gradual accumulation of items which they cannot buy all at once. These consist of home furnishings, appliances, wall hangings and pictures, musical instruments, books for a library, and other items. Some items may be in the luxury category, and it is important not to go into debt for these. In fact, think carefully before acquiring any debts at all. In this day of easy charge accounts, many couples get too deeply in debt before they realize it. Start a savings or investment program in the first year.

Conflict arises when one spouse wants an item of considerable expense and the other would like for the money to be spent in a different way. In one case a marriage almost broke up when the husband, as he put it, "fell in love with a sports car," which the wife said they didn't need and couldn't afford. Here we see the need for joint decisions on major expenditures. As far as possible, however, let your budget make decisions for you. It will make the marriage start out and run much more smoothly.

Money isn't everything, but it is a very visible item on the marriage agenda, and the decision on how to use it comes up every day. Good earning, spending, and saving habits started at the very beginning of married life will bring rich rewards in the years to come.

More than almost anything else, your checkbook record will give concrete evidence as to what your real value system is. Couples with similar values will find married life much simpler and easier to negotiate because your values will guide you in the same direction toward the same goals. You cannot separate the material (the things you want) from the spiritual (your values).

Why are the first months of marriage so important? The first steps create a path that the couple will move in, perhaps for the rest of their lives. If the first steps are faulty, the music may stop and the couple will cease dancing altogether. A number of studies show that marriages that end in divorce do so within a two-year period. The average elapsed time until the divorce is granted is about seven years, and this has not changed in one hundred years.[4] If a couple has a happy adjustment over the first two years, such is a good indication that the marriage will last. If the first seven years are happy ones, the chance of failure diminishes rapidly. So, it all begins in those first important steps in the "marriage dance."

Suggested Activity for Chapter 8

1. The tune to which you measure your "life dance" may be determined by your value system. Read Matthew 6:25-33 and discuss how this passage might apply to the importance of compatible values systems in the "marriage dance."
2. Most married couples need to create more fun and joy in their marriage and family life. Note references to the importance of this in John 15:10,11; and John 16:33. What are the messages for you?
3. Construct a budget in which each of you indicates those items that are essential and those that are "nice but not necessary." Discuss your similarities and differences in deciding on essentials and their importance.
4. Discuss the meaning of the word "stewardship" and how it might affect your concept of possessions. What percentage of income should a couple set aside for giving to a church or to charitable causes?

CHAPTER *9*

Who Am I and What Am I Supposed to Do?

Getting married brings about a great many changes and raises a number of questions about who you are and what you are supposed to do. Decisions about very simple things can come into play. When I was moderator of a talk show on a television station in the Midwest some years ago, my guests and I were discussing the process by which husbands and wives decide how household responsibilities can be divided. A viewer called in at this point and said the following: "My wife is sitting next to me watching this program, and I want you to tell her that it is not the husband's job to take out the trash!" What amused me about this request was that I always considered it was my duty to take out the trash at our house. I tried to be diplomatic in my answer and not alienate him altogether by saying, "It is really a matter to work out with one's spouse, and I do not think it inappropriate for either one of you to take out the trash."

Sometimes I try to think back on the first weeks and months of my own marriage in order to appreciate what it means to make this major transition in one's life. There are so many new experiences to negotiate and so many challenges to meet. And many of us do all this when we are still young and immature. It is remarkable that couples do as well as they do under these circumstances.

As I have observed couples getting married and starting life together, I have concluded that in most cases it is a greater adjustment for the wife than for the husband. In many instances the man will be working before the marriage takes place. After the wedding, and perhaps a honeymoon, he goes back to life as usual. How about the woman? She may have been finishing her education, or working at a job, and now she becomes—for the first time in her life—a housewife. This is very different! Some women have had some previous experience in the homes from which they come or in an apartment of their own, doing some cooking, cleaning, and perhaps some purchasing. Now a much greater responsibility is placed on her shoulders. She must adjust to a new way of life. Even though she may be working at a job outside the home, she is still considered in many cases to be the housewife and homemaker. I have had women clients tell me that they work forty hours at an outside job, come home and cook the meals and do most of the household chores. This means about a sixty-five-hour workweek.

Fortunately, men are beginning to realize that this is unfair and that they have an obligation to help their wives adjust to their new lifestyle and take on their fair share of household responsibilities. The same thing is true when it comes to child care, which we will discuss later in chapter 15. If marriage is to be a partnership, then all responsibilities must be shared so as to serve the best interests of both partners.

Getting married is a transition into an intimacy that two people have never known before. It is not only a new situation, but a new relationship. All of us come from families where we live in proximity with parents, brothers, and sisters. If one is an only child, then he or she is deprived of the give-and-take experience that only siblings can know about. In other words, most of us go into marriage out of social situations. We are partly socialized, and this helps. However, marriage is the first intimate heterosexual relationship for most of us. Here are a male and female living together under the same roof. Perhaps gender identity, the questions about who I am and who you are come to the surface in a way that they never have before. We are together in the kitchen, the dining room, the living room, the bedroom, and elsewhere, trying to discover who we are and what we are supposed to do in all of these situations.

This raises questions about femininity and masculinity. What does it mean to be a woman? What does it mean to be a man? We do not look the same. We are physiologically different. Is anatomy our destiny? This is a question that is being discussed widely at the present time. We might begin thinking about this by taking a look at some of the traditional ways of looking at gender identity. We develop self-concepts by learning what others think we are supposed to be and imitating others who serve as models for us. We are often told what we are supposed to be and how we are supposed to act. Perhaps our parents told us, "Girls do this and don't do that!" Or, "This is what boys are supposed to do, and they are never supposed to do that!" Little girls are given dolls; little boys are given trucks and baseball gloves. Girls may have the privilege of crying. Boys should never cry! Girls should grow up to be young women who are warm, gentle, compassionate, maternal, and helpful. Boys should grow up to be strong, tough, aggressive, cool, protective, and use words sparingly. So we are told!

A look at how concepts have developed and changed through the years will help us understand ourselves more fully. If you had a chance to ask your grandmother or grandfather what they thought the differences were or ought to be, what do you suppose they would have told you? How different would they be from what you might think today? No doubt, they would describe the male and female in very traditional terms. What do you think your parents would say in answer to a question about masculinity and femininity? Would their concepts have changed from that of your grandparents?

Margaret Mead suggested that sex differences are largely due to environmental influences. However, researchers currently are discovering that a great many sex differences are due to physiological causes. So in order to understand one another, we must resort to a number of findings from neurologists, biochemists, endocrinologists, psychologists, sociologists, parents, and educators. It seems to me that this is an area in which there is a great deal of ignorance and one in which people need to become more informed in order to understand and communicate better with the opposite sex. If that came to pass, those of us in the marital counseling field would have fewer people coming to us saying, "I don't understand my wife!" "I don't understand my husband!" Or, "Why are women this way?" Or, "Why are men like that?"

What are some of the differences to consider that might help us to be more sensitive in understanding our spouses and thereby be able to communicate and relate more effectively? First, let us agree that differences do not mean inequality. We are different because of nature or nurture. If we are considered unequal as sexes, it is due to a political, ethical, or ideological distortion.

When you are first married, you will notice some of the differences. For instance, if a wife wants a heavy object lifted, she may expect her husband to lift it. He will probably be physically stronger. This is because he has more muscle. However, on a shopping tour the husband may tire long before his wife, partly due to psychological causes, but mostly because women have more stamina than men. This is partly due to the fact that women have a larger percentage of fat and less muscle tissue, which gives them the extra stamina. Dr. Joan W. L. Ullyot, formerly of the Institute of Health Research in San Francisco, concluded that endurance is the key in long-distance athletic events, and that women generally have greater endurance than men. This is due to the fact that muscles depend on the carbohydrate-storing substance called glycogen for fuel. This works well for a short period, but it doesn't last long. After an athlete has run a long distance, the glycogen is consumed, and the body switches over to fat as its main source of energy. Since fat yields about seven times as much energy per gram as glycogen does, it is a more efficient fuel, and more available for women. Glycogen is sometimes referred to as "animal starch." So if you are a man and your wife chides you for running out of steam before she does, you can now say, "You and your fat!"

If we study the comparative strengths of the two sexes, the old macho image of the strong male and the weak female goes down the drain. Women seem to be more able to endure pain, illness, fatigue, and infection, and, of course, they live longer—about eight years longer on the average than men. If you marry a man who is the same age or older, dear wife, remember that you have a good chance of being a widow. This should have some effect on your insurance and financial planning program.

Because much study recently has been given to the nature of the brain, we know a great deal more about the differences between the male and female brain. A girl's left brain (which controls speech) develops more rapidly than a boy's. A boy's right brain (which controls vision) develops more rapidly than a girl's. These tend to catch up later, but many neurologists are beginning to believe that these differences cause different kinds of functions in males and females. For example, men seem to function in a more specialized way; they are more detailed and analytical. Women function in a more generalized fashion, which seems to make them more perceptive. Women take in the whole picture. This may account for the fact that women are attributed with the gift of "intuition." Another theory is that men tend to use the right brain when dealing with spatial problems and the left for verbal problems, while women work with the right and left hemispheres of the brain together. No doubt, we will know much about this as new research reveals it.

Do these differences have any effect on the way a husband and wife communicate? My experience as a marital therapist would lead me to believe that women would like more communication with their husbands. Alice came in one day complaining, "How can I get Bill to put down his newspaper and talk with me?" If women are more verbally developed than men, this is a factor men need to take into consideration. From the very beginning of their marriages, men should concentrate more on listening to and talking with their wives. They should also practice expressing their feelings, which some men are reluctant to do.

What about sexual differences in lovemaking? Is there a biological difference here? The hormonal structure is certainly different, and this may cause some misunderstanding. Men tend to be more aggressive and women more passive, although this has as much to do with past conditioning as it has to do with hormones or brain function. Women need a longer time to become sexually aroused than men, as a rule, and that needs to be carefully understood. Polly, a recently married young woman, came to me recently and asked, "Can't you do something with my husband? He just doesn't understand that I need a considerable amount of caring, caressing, and loving before we have sexual intercourse." Many women feel that the closeness, the intimacy, the cuddling, and the caring are the most important matters in the sexual act. Once she is sexually aroused, the woman generally has more capacity to enjoy sex than a man, and certainly over a longer period of time.

I received an interesting letter from a couple who had been married for only a short time. One line read: "Every person in the world is different from everyone else. And to think you can put two of these different people together in a marriage and they will get along!" Yes, it is marvelous that this can happen. Perhaps it is because we can understand and accept these differences. Over a period of time we can adjust to them. We can change for the better if that is necessary. Because of our nature and our nurture we will bring a variety of characteristics into our marriages. It is hoped that the variety will make for richness and excitement in the relationship rather than conflict.

Let us return to the talk show incident where the husband asked me to tell his wife that men are not supposed to carry out the trash. What was wrong here? For one thing, he carried into his marriage preconceived ideas about men's roles and women's roles. I daresay he was a rigid person and gave his wife problems in areas other than trash disposal. There was a time when roles were fairly closely defined. One hundred years ago over 90 percent of the people in this country lived on farms and ranches. In rural life almost everyone in the family had a specified role to perform, or else the farm would not function. The father was in the field, the mother was in the kitchen, and the children each had certain tasks to perform. Today more than 90 percent of all people live in large towns or cities. For the most part, the traditional family does not exist. Most women will work outside the home sometime during their lifetime. The extended family where parents and relatives lived in the same neighborhood is gone. All of us live in a highly industrialized society which makes demands on us unheard of by our grandparents. The so-called "home industry" production of former years—raising fruits and vegetables, canning, weaving, tailoring, repairing, carpentry, and related activities—are no longer considered a necessity by most families. If any of these is practiced, it is done so as art or recreation rather than as a necessity for family survival.

It is my contention that differences can enrich a marriage, but these differences must have a complimentary rather than a conflicting effect. It is up to the couple to see that differences are modified so as to be compatible. Also, I am not so concerned about which spouse has a particular characteristic or which spouse plays a particular role. Men should be free to show their feelings and cry when it helps to do so; women should be free to be assertive, to express their need for love, and to assume leadership when it is called for. Men should take responsibility for their share of housework and child care. Women need not be afraid to have a career or fix the kitchen faucet. It is all right for men to be tender, warm, compassionate, and romantic. It is good for women to be active in politics, community affairs, and athletics. There is an interesting word in the dictionary—"androgynous." It denotes having both male and female characteristics. This does not mean "unisex" — indistinguishable on the basis of gender. I do not want to see men and women become alike, indistinguishable. However, I do not want anyone to feel that he or she cannot express a true and genuine trait or feeling because of some traditional male or female stereotype. As a couple begins their life together in marriage, let them keep this kind of flexibility in mind.

Should the husband be considered the predominant breadwinner and the wife the predominant homemaker? Most of the couples in my successful marriage study would answer, "Yes!" And yet many of the wives in that group do work outside the home. Many of them work to help give the family a better standard of living. Some of them have careers. Some of them work off and on. Some have started work or a career after the children have left home. In several cases, the wife supported the family while the husband finished his education. I believe they would all say that if children are going to be brought into the home, they must have the kind of care that is best for their development. I am not sure this can come to pass if both partners are engaged full-time in pursuing a career that takes them out of the home for most of the day. We know that infants require specialized, sensitive, skillful, and loving care during the first years of their lives. They need someone who understands their uniqueness and special needs. The mother and the father are in the best position to do this. It is highly unlikely that a substitute could be found to fulfill this function. If one parent could be at home while the other worked, I think the needs of the infant could be met. This does not preclude having both parents work, but it would mean one or both might have to work part-time. The nurture and development of children must have one of the highest priorities in a family and in society. I am not sure that this is so at the present time.

In the busy life that most couples have today, many functions in the home must be shared. I don't advocate that either one should be boss, or head of the house, but I do insist that there be an agreement on a division of labor. This means that each must assume responsibility for certain tasks that must be done if the marriage and the family are to function. Perhaps we need to be more businesslike in running our households. At the beginning of a marriage, a couple should sit down and map out a plan for operating a household. At one time I made a list of all the vocational skills and accomplishments that go into making a home function. When I was through, I had thirty-five categories on my list, and I am sure there must be more. Who does what, when, and where? Use the following aid to help you decide.

Role Concept Comparison[1]

Use the inventory on the following page to evaluate your degree of agreement on roles in married life. Key: *a*—definitely agree; *b*—agree with reservations; *c*—not sure; *d*—tend to disagree; *e*—definitely disagree. Indicate your choice in the column of the appropriate letter.

Female | | | | | | | **Male**
a	b	c	d	e		a	b	c	d	e

1. The husband is head of the family.
2. The status of the wife should be that of "junior partner."
3. Wives should feel free to have a career.
4. The mother has the greater responsibility for children.
5. The husband should be the major source of financial support.
6. The mother should be home most of the time until the last child enters school or preschool.
7. The father is equally responsible for homemaking and the care of children.
8. Marriage should be thought of as an equal partnership.
9. The husband and wife should go to church together.
10. The couple (or family) should eat out once a week.
11. The husband and wife should plan the budget, manage money, and keep accurate financial records together.
12. Neither should purchase an item costing over $100 without consulting the other.
13. The wife should feel free to initiate lovemaking with her husband.
14. The wife should always have the house neat and clean.
15. Husbands should be mostly responsible for the "instrumental" dimensions of marriage (financial, physical labor, repair work, and so forth).
16. Wives should be mostly responsible for the "expressive" dimensions (compassion, affection, caring, nursing, and so forth).
17. The wife is primarily responsible for "birth control."
18. Kitchen responsibilities (cooking, cleaning, dish washing, and so forth) should be shared by husband and wife.
19. Each spouse should have areas in which he or she is mostly responsible for decision making.
20. It is all right for men to cry if they feel like it.
21. Most young people get very poor training for parenthood.
22. Too much television viewing can prevent couples from important companionship with each other.
23. A good practice to start in the early days of marriage is setting aside a certain time each week for discussing household matters, finance, and making plans.
24. Daily devotions, Bible reading, and prayer will enhance a marriage.

Suggested Activity for Chapter 9

1. Ask your parents and/or your grandparents what they think are distinctive characteristics of a man and of a woman. How are your ideas similar or different?
2. If you are in a serious relationship or married to another person, take the role concept test in this chapter and compare results. If there is no partner in your life now, complete your portion and let someone comment on the results.
3. List the feminine and masculine characteristics that you see in each other. Are these traditional? Contemporary? How do you react to what you see in each other?

CHAPTER *10*

The Icing on the Wedding Cake

Why did I choose such a title for this chapter? I have tasted a great many wedding cakes during the past years. I would estimate that I have had a slice from a thousand cakes or more. They came in all sizes and shapes; were mostly white with a tiny bride and groom on top; and contained a variety of ingredients which determined qualities ranging from "one bite is enough" to "I'd like a second helping." They all had one thing in common — icing. Wedding cakes do not have to have icing, but they all do. Why? There is something about the icing that adds to the enjoyment of the cake. And icing made out of pure ingredients — butter, sugar, egg whites, and so forth — is delicious, indeed. However, it would not be a good idea to eat the icing apart from the cake, would it? The icing performs a very important function when it is eaten with the cake.

This analogy can be applied to sex in marriage. The cake, the wedding of two people, is good in itself. It consists of many of the ingredients mentioned in previous chapters that provide a good "mix" for a well-functioning relationship. Add to this the icing—the sexual relationship—and there is an extra something that brings added beauty, pleasure, excitement, and satisfaction. Sex without a loving relationship, as I see it, is like eating icing without the cake—sweet at first, but quickly losing its appeal and likely to lead to indigestion. However, when the right amount of good quality sex is added to the relationship, and it is integrated into the whole, the result is very satisfying and lasting.

What is the deeper meaning of sex, and what function does it perform? Let us turn to two passages in the book of Genesis. The first is Genesis 2, verses 24 and 25: "Therefore a man leaves his father and mother and cleaves to his wife, and they become one flesh. And the man and his wife were both naked, and were not ashamed." This implies the complete union that marriage makes possible. Separately, male and female are incomplete. They are incomplete physically, mentally, and spiritually. There is a loneliness in this incompleteness. God's intention for life is that relationships be formed. "You shall love the Lord your God with all your heart . . . and you shall love your neighbor as yourself" (Matthew 22:37,39). In this vertical and horizontal relationship are peace and harmony. Companionship is the answer to loneliness. The ultimate in companionship is marriage, where two "become one flesh." This union is realized when the two are together in mind, body, and spirit.

As I pointed out in a previous chapter, the *eros* kind of love is more than sexual desire; it is a total binding of two people out of their desire to become one flesh. It is a mental, physical, and spiritual bonding—a combination of cake and icing. This is why sexual intercourse takes on a much deeper and more profound meaning in marriage.

The second reference is in Genesis 4:1: "Now Adam knew his wife, and she conceived and bore Cain, saying, 'I have gotten a man with the help of the Lord.' " The word "know" (yadá) is used in the Old Testament to indicate the sexual act. It is interesting that a physical symbol is not chosen, but a mental and spiritual symbol — "to know." It is mental in that here one recognizes and acknowledges the presence of the other person. It is spiritual in that it is "knowing from the inside,"[1] as Thielicke puts it. This is a special kind of knowledge which probes into the mystery of the other. To this extent, sexual intercourse can become a unique form of communication that is only accessible to two people joined in body, mind, and spirit. At the same time it may partake of the purpose of divine creation: "I have gotten a man with the help of the Lord." It is important to see that God is recognized as a part of this creative process. Children are conceived and born and become the next generation, and the human race is preserved. Now we can begin to see the profound and far-reaching nature of sexual relations.

In contrast, we recognize the superficial and crass portrayal of such an important phenomenon in much of the contemporary media: movies, books, magazines, television, and the theater. Because we are bombarded with this misleading propaganda day after day, wherever we go, it is little wonder that couples enter marriage confused as to what sex means or should contribute to their relationship. It is time to clarify this matter as best we can so that more couples will have a better chance to develop a satisfactory and permanent relationship in married life. When a couple engage in sexual intercourse, they may experience any or all of the following:

1. A very satisfactory and pleasurable experience.
2. A feeling of being loving and loved.
3. A cooperative venture in bringing a new life into the world.
4. A deeper experience of knowing each other; breaking through mysterious boundaries.
5. An escape from loneliness into unity and wholeness.
6. The joy of giving completely of oneself.
7. A release from tension and an experience of complete relaxation.
8. An adventure in discovering new ways of bringing joy and satisfaction to each other.
9. A way of engaging in adult play and having fun together.

The list could go on and on. Couples just entering marriage could learn much from other couples like those in my study of successful marriages. They have allowed me to look into their personal lives to see the variety of sexual experiences revealed there. From them I have learned better how to help others overcome some of their fears and anxieties and reassure them that it is possible to have a complete marriage in which sex plays an important role. I will share some of these insights in the following paragraphs.

What are some of the problems that newly married couples face in terms of their sexual relationships? People come into a marriage bringing with them a considerable amount of ideas, attitudes, and feelings about sex. These begin in infancy and develop through all the years preceding the marriage. Parents consciously and unconsciously form the first impressions of gender identity in a child's mind. A child's disposition, be it warm and loving or cold and withdrawn, begins in its relationship to mother and then father, followed by others. This may be the most important factor in one's sexual development. As time goes on, the child learns attitudes toward bodily functions and the opposite sex. It is rare to find a parent who is also a good sex educator. This role begins early and requires some expertise in communication skills with children.

It was here that Sherrie first ran into trouble.[2] She came to me several months before her marriage expressing her fear and anxiety about sex as it might occur in her future marriage. In her childhood experience in home and school she got the impression that sex was dirty and animalistic. All that her mother ever taught her was to be careful of boys, "they could get you into trouble," and over and above all, she must never get pregnant before marriage. And that was about all she heard.

Sherrie came for a series of sessions in which she talked about all her problems and what she might do to overcome them. We discussed the positive aspects of sex and how she might develop new attitudes to take into her marriage. The man she would marry was in Europe but through letters he came to understand her problem.

After marriage she wrote me a letter, hoping that her experience might be of help to others. Because of the counseling and the patience and love of her husband, she wrote, she overcame her problems and developed a healthy sexual relationship in her marriage. However, it took ten months of marriage to do it. She wanted others to know that it is never too late to change feelings and attitudes, overcome early negative experiences of sex, and enter into a satisfactory sex life after marriage. She also had something to say to other young women, with experiences similar to hers, about guilt. Sherrie entered marriage as a virgin, which made her, as some might say, sexually inexperienced. Immediately upon being married, all restraints were off, and she was expected to be completely uninhibited. This, she said, was difficult for her to accomplish. She kept feeling guilty about being so sexually free. And she still had to do battle with the idea that there was something wrong with having sex. Sherrie was a devoutly religious young woman, and it took her awhile to reconcile her religious beliefs about morality and her new sexual life. This, too, she relates, can be done. She did accomplish such a reconciliation. She sees sex, in context, as a divinely planned function for humans to practice and enjoy.

Every young couple can expect to go through a series of adjustments in developing a sexual style that will be meaningful to both. Bessie and Ted came to my office with a problem that arose in the first few weeks of their marriage regarding frequency of intercourse. Ted thought twice a day was not too often. Bessie thought once a week was normal. I began by explaining that couples should discuss this together and arrive at a compromise with which they could both live. I knew the statistics and suggested they start their discussion from there. The frequency during the first year averages three times a week. It is less after children come, and by age forty it falls to once a week.[3] (Bessie was acting twenty years too soon.) They need not accept the average if it did not fit their particular needs. Bessie and Ted were now more able to reach a satisfactory solution, which has worked very well for them.

Ethel and Byron came in expressing disagreements about coital positions and techniques. I explained that the solution was not a matter of finding the "right" positions or techniques, which can vary considerably from couple to couple, but in finding those that were most satisfactory for both of them. I loaned them a book I thought might be helpful, explaining that books are not the answer to such problems, but I was in favor of young couples being well-informed through reading as well as experimentation. Seminars and study groups dealing with sexuality in marriage can also be helpful.

Some couples expect too much from their sexual life all the time. Experiences will vary from time to time. The ringing of bells and the flashing of colored lights may occur now and then, but not all the time. There will be times when one or the other is disappointed, but this mustn't be discouraging. There are times when one or the other is not in the mood, a situation that should be respected. Culprits that are most apt to steal sexual enjoyment away from the couple are fear, fatigue, resentment, and unresolved conflict. Every marital therapist knows that people with sexual problems are likely to be having interpersonal problems. Misunderstandings, anger, resentment, hostility, and poor communication will make a good sexual experience difficult. Joanne complained in a counseling session, "How can we expect to quarrel all day and be compatible in bed at night?" Of course she and her husband couldn't.

On the other hand, couples who have learned to solve their problems, resolve their conflicts, control their anger, deal with resentment, and show love in doing so seem to handle their sexual relations quite well. They are proficient communicators who know how to express their feelings, needs, and expectations. They don't expect their spouses to be mind readers. They are in sync with each other all the way through.

Are there differences in sexual natures that make it difficult for a satisfactory adjustment? In the previous chapter I attempted to explain the differences between male and female and also the differences in each in relation to others of their own sex. We aren't sure about what has been called a "sexual drive," but we do know that there are differences in sexual desires and needs in people. I have worked with couples whose desires and needs were far apart, but who through an understanding of each other were able to work out a satisfactory relationship. Some individuals are more warm and loving than their spouses, and this means quite an adjustment on the part of less affectionate spouses to learn to be loving. Some are more aggressive, some more passive, some more traditional, some more given to experimentation. These differences are not impossible to overcome. Again, it means understanding, communicating, and negotiating a solution.

Married life is quite complicated in these modern times and consists of many activities and events. There are many passages and transitions as time goes on requiring many types of adjustment in a relationship which includes sexual relations. When children come, life is never the same until they fly out of the nest. It seems that there are more things to occupy the time of parents, and life gets busier and busier. Sexual relations have to find their proper place among all the other matters of married life. Someone has figured that during the first year of marriage, an average couple will spend about one hundred fifty hours in sexual intercourse, but over two thousand hours in doing all kinds of other things. In my research project, I discovered that couples in the first year or two of marriage concentrated on developing a high degree of satisfaction in their sexual relations. As time went on, some were able to maintain this level, while others tapered off and found greater interest in other areas of their lives. Sexual satisfaction is in the perception of it by each partner, just as beauty is in the eye of the beholder.

After getting married, some couples develop serious sexual problems. Those experienced by the male are premature ejaculation, impotency (erectile dysfunctions), and, occasionally, inhibited sexual desire. Those associated with females are failure to achieve orgasm, vaginismus (spastic reaction in the vagina to being penetrated), total anorgasticity (void of sexual feelings), and inhibited sexual desire or sexual aversion. When these occur, the couple should go to a clinical sexual therapist for assistance. The major causes of serious sexual difficulty are found not in the physiological area but arise out of various kinds of fear, insecurity, hostility, and guilt. The prognostic indicators for improvement for any sexual problems depend on the short duration of the problem, the presence of sexual desire on the part of both spouses, the feelings of love they have for each other, the willingness on the part of both to cooperate with and help each other, the absence of psychopathology, the motivation to work to improve the situation, and an otherwise happy marriage.

I mentioned earlier that some of the problems couples have in the first year of their marriages are due to ignorance (Bessie and Ted's case) or assuming some myths to be true (Sherrie's case). My experience tells me that many couples go into marriage with an inadequate knowledge of anatomy and the various uses of contraceptive devices. A basic knowledge of male and female anatomy would help in understanding how each other functions. A competent gynecologist can help a couple understand the pros and cons of the various contraceptive devices, and a visit with him or her is a must.

Myths still prevail in spite of refutations by eminent specialists in the field of sexuality. These myths include (1) men know all that is necessary about sex and are the best teachers for their wives. (Tests that I have given to males through the years prove they are woefully ignorant in many important areas.) (2) Pain and bleeding are signs of female virginity. (If difficulty is present in the first experience of intercourse, it is usually due to inadequate arousal or anxiety.) (3) The size of the sex organs have a lot to do with sexual compatibility or satisfaction. (As the excitement stage phases into the plateau stage, the sexual organs are of a relatively equal size in all persons.) (4) Men need to reach the stage of orgasm, but women do not. (After a female has reached the plateau stage and does not have an orgasm, she may experience discomfort or even pain for several hours.) (5) To be clean and dainty and hold her husband's love, a woman should have internal cleansing. (Millions of dollars are being made on the myth that women should use a particular douching solution. A shower with mild soap and water is sufficient preparation.) (6) It is not necessary to know the various stages of progress in sexual intercourse; just let nature take its course. (It is very helpful to know the four stages and the function of each: Excitement, Plateau, Orgasm, Resolution.[4] Also, it helps to know how men and women may function differently in each stage.) (7) It is possible to purchase aphrodisiacs to enhance sexual performance. (They are of no value and may be dangerous. Hormones and minor tranquilizers may be of some help in a small percentage of cases). (8) Alcohol or drugs will make sexual relations more pleasurable. (Very doubtful. As Shakespeare wrote: "It provokes the desire, but takes away the performance.") (9) The most desirable female orgasm should take place in the vagina rather than in the clitoris. (This is a discarded Freudian notion.) (10) Simultaneous orgasm should be sought by all couples as the ultimate sexual experience. (Rarely achieved, and not necessary.)

Couples should enter marriage with realistic expectations for sexual satisfaction. Some seem to achieve it in a relatively short time. Some take years. Some make it hard work rather than the fun and play that it should be. A good sense of humor also helps. My four key words for sexual achievement are: Passion, Practice, Patience, and Persistence. Mix these with a lot of love, and I think you will make it.

Let me sum up this chapter by stating some characteristics I have seen in the happy couples I have been studying for the past thirteen years. These traits seem to have had a profound effect on their ability to achieve sexual fulfillment in themselves and in their partners.[5]

1. The partners are warm, friendly, outgoing.

2. They are generous, unselfish, and enjoy giving other people pleasure.
3. They are physically and emotionally healthy: active, energetic, and fun-loving, with a good sense of humor.
4. They are good communicators, letting their feelings be known, skillful in managing conflict and settling differences. They are able to deal with anger and resentment.
5. They enjoy being themselves, like their femininity and masculinity, and have an adequate level of self-esteem.
6. They have a positive attitude toward sex and sexual functions and enjoy closeness and intimacy.
7. They have a high regard for sexual relations and think of them as God-given functions for the human race to express physical, mental, and spiritual union.
8. They are loyal, faithful, dependable, and are able to instill trust and respect in their partners.
9. They are altogether mentally, morally, emotionally, and spiritually healthy individuals.

Such people seem to know a lot about "wedding cake," the delicious "icing" that goes with it, and how to put the two together.

Suggested Activity for Chapter 10

1. Read the first four chapters of Genesis in the Bible. Why did God create the human race as male and female?
2. Distinguish between human beings and animals in regard to their sexual natures and behavior. Why do we apply the word "moral" or "immoral" to human behavior but not to animal behavior?
3. Review several current popular magazines. Find some articles on sex, love, and marriage. What are the articles attempting to say about these subjects? Cut out illustrations in the advertisements that portray some concepts of sex or love. Evaluate.
4. Read the nine characteristics of a competent sexual partner. What are your strengths? What are your growth areas? Read each and answer for yourself.

CHAPTER *11*

I Promised You a
Rose Garden

Every couple who ever got married had some vision or dream of what life would be like after the wedding. Happiness, satisfaction, personal fulfillment, companionship, children to make the family complete—all these things were beckoning lights inviting the couple into the future. I have observed hundreds of couples on the threshold of marriage. For the most part they are radiantly happy, anticipating the future optimistically, eagerly planning their lives together. They might be compared to candidates running for office and picturing the future where peace and plenty will abound once they are in office. Campaign promises fill the air: "Marry me and I will make you the happiest person in the world, and love in all its glory will prevail."

Then what happens? Almost half of these couples fail to achieve a state that would cause them to want to live together more than a few years. The beautifully decorated wedding cake crumbles. The rose garden wilts, withers, and dies. Why does such a promising start end in this sorry state? Our gardener recently told us the story of a family in our community who had great plans for a beautiful layout of trees, flowers, and shrubs. They spent a considerable amount of money buying these items from a local nursery and planting them. When one plants anything in the desert, great care must be taken to dig a hole the proper size and to replace the sand and gravel with nourishing top soil. After the plant is securely in place, it must be watered and fertilized at proper intervals. In this family's case, two mistakes were made—the holes were not dug deeply enough for proper drainage, and the plantings were neglected after they were put in the ground. All of this began in the springtime. The summer came with its blistering hot sun. By late fall most of the plants were dead. The gardener shook his head, saying, "What a pity to let that happen! They could have had a beautiful garden."

This might be considered a parable of many marriages. Everything seems very promising in the springtime. Friends say good things about the couple at the wedding—how charming they are, how beautiful the bride, how handsome the groom, how happy they will be. They are whisked away to their honeymoon amid showers of rice and shouts of good luck and best wishes. Weeks go by, then months, and the marriage begins to wilt. It stops growing and starts dying. Is this caused by poor stock, improper nourishment, neglect, or all three?

There are a multitude of causes for marital malfunctioning. Some people are poor prospects for marriage; they perform inadequately in interpersonal relationships. Sometimes two people are good prospects for marriage, but not for each other; if they marry, they will form a misalliance and end up disliking each other. Then there are some who are adequate for marriage and could be compatible with each other, but they behave in a manner that causes conflict and disruption. And there are others who neglect the marriage, who do nothing to enrich it that it might grow; so it withers and dies. What might have been a beautiful rose garden ends up a weed patch.

Let us return to the Genesis story once again, focusing on chapter 3. Adam, the man, and Eve, the woman, were joined together in a permanent relationship we call marriage. They were given an environment in which all things necessary for their well-being were available. This can best be described as a garden. In this story it is called the Garden of Eden. The garden signified God's intention for his creation—love, beauty, peace, and a bountiful supply of food. This garden, like all gardens, had certain principles that had to be taken into consideration if all things were to prosper. The garden had its privileges, and it had its restrictions. The symbol for the restrictions was a particular tree. It might have been a bed of flowers in which there was a sign, "Don't gather these flowers!" Or it might have been a lovely lawn with a sign, "Keep off the grass!" It happened to be a tree, and on it there may have been a sign, "Don't pick the fruit." Now there was plenty of fruit in the garden. When Eve was tempted by the serpent, she countered with, "We may eat of the fruit of the trees of the garden, but God said, 'You shall not eat of the fruit of the tree which is in the midst of the garden, neither shall you touch it, lest you die.' " But the tempter replied, "You will not die. For God knows that when you eat of it, your eyes will be opened, and you will be like God, knowing good and evil." At this point the process of rationalization began. "So when the woman saw that the tree was good for food, and that it was a delight to the eyes, and the tree was to be desired to make one wise, she took of its fruit and ate, and she also gave some to her husband, and he ate. Then the eyes of both were opened, and they knew they were naked . . ." (Genesis 3:2-7, paraphrased).

What followed is interesting, indeed. God came looking for Adam, and called, "Where are you?" Adam tried to hide, and when God found him, Adam offered a ridiculous excuse: "I was afraid, because I was naked; and I hid myself." God got right to the crux of the matter: "Who told you that you were naked? Have you eaten of the tree of which I commanded you not to eat?" Adam was caught; what could he do? Maybe this would work: "The woman whom thou gavest to be with me, she gave me fruit of the tree, and I ate." Now what could Eve do about this little game her husband was playing? She said, "The serpent beguiled me, and I ate." This is the first account on record of what is now called "passing the buck." Also, something else is implied here. Thielicke says this represents "a disruption in the order of creation."[1] God intended this bonded couple to be "one flesh." This perfect union was partially severed by a struggle on the part of each to escape responsibility by shifting the blame. Each tried to protect himself and herself at the expense of the other, as if thinking, *What does it matter what happens to the other person, as long as I save myself?* God might have said, "Let us forget the whole thing. Please don't do it again." No, God could not do that in the face of a violation of one of the basic principles of the garden. Forgiveness is always possible, but one must accept the consequences of his or her acts. As in the case of the family that lost their garden through poor planting and neglect, the garden was lost. As for Adam and Eve, life would never be the same again. They were forced to move to another location which might be called "East Eden." Life there was not as easy. All was not beautiful, and food came only as the result of the "sweat of the brow."

Regardless of how you interpret this story in the book of Genesis, you need to see it as a parable of human life and relationships, a realm where the possibilities are so great. The potential of all creation is astounding. If all people treated the land as a sacred trust, there would be no ugliness in nature, and all would have sufficient food to eat. If human potential were fully realized, think what a paradise this world would be! If people related to one another as God intended, there would be no hate, no violence, no war. We would live in love and the world would be a neighborhood. Marriage would be a state in which we could find perpetual joy. This is a promise. This is the order of creation. However, essence and existence are not the same. What we could be and what we are seem worlds apart. Why? We all have a gift that can be a blessing or a liability. It is called freedom. This is what makes us human and sets us apart from most of the rest of creation. We are free to choose. And we can choose good or evil. We are even free to deny our Maker. We are not free, however, to escape the consequences of our actions.

Why would anyone violate any of the principles that make for healthy growth in the garden? When one can act to create happiness, why should he or she act to bring misery? I believe that the fundamental cause of most of this misery is due to a person's tendency to be preoccupied with his or her own self-interests. When one serves his or her own interests at the expense of another's, dissension and trouble come.

Let us take a look at what this selfish tendency does to marriage. Harry first came in with Marie for marriage counseling when Marie threatened to leave him if he refused. They had been married twenty-five years and had three children, two of them still at home. During the year following the first session, they have been back many times. Marie's complaint at the beginning was that Harry was too busy with his business affairs and in the organizations to which he belonged to pay much attention to her. I have come to know them both very well. Marie tends to complain too much and needs extra reinforcement to maintain her self-esteem. On the other hand, Harry tends to get wrapped up in his own interests and concerns, which causes Marie to feel neglected. When they first came for help, I discovered that Harry had not taken Marie out to a movie or dinner for months. They had not gone anywhere together except to church, which Harry finally stopped attending because he said it was boring. Harry made important decisions and bought expensive items without consulting Marie. His own interests became so important to him that he neglected to give proper attention to those of his wife and children. His garden was beginning to wither from lack of nourishment and neglect.

In our Genesis story, Adam and Eve brought trouble into their lives when they put their own interests ("the tree was good for food, and . . . it was a delight to the eyes, and that the tree was desired to make one wise,") ahead of what God intended for them to do. He promised them a garden to enjoy if they would act responsibly within it.

Theologians sometimes talk of original sin, referring to mankind's sinful nature. This was never very clear to me until I began to observe the way some people acted, particularly in marriage. Happiness is a promise to every couple if they will love each other and not violate their freedom by disrupting the order of creation. However, we are all prone to think of ourselves first. I call this the "egocentric predicament." As I see it, this is not the essence of what we are supposed to be. It is a violation of this essence. It negates the promise that the two shall become one flesh. As I see so many unhappy couples coming into my office, I say to myself, "Why do they insist on being miserable when they could be happy?"

Harry was causing a lot of unhappiness in his home because he was putting his own interests ahead of those of all other family members. Now he had to change. The therapy consisted of the family working together to bring this about, with Harry taking the lead. And things did improve when Harry became aware of what was happening to the marriage and his responsibility in helping to change it.

When couples first get married, it is easy for each to get caught up in his or her own world of concerns and demands. They need to put high on their list of priorities the resolve to continue what was started in courtship, i.e., a genuine desire to help each other, do thoughtful things, encourage, reinforce, and love each other every day. Remember how all these things put together made you want to marry in the first place and have a beautiful rose garden?

It has been said of politicians that they construct platforms to help them step into office. Once in, they often forget the platform. Young newlyweds, don't forget your promises, the platform you built together. And don't forget what God has prepared for you if you are willing to receive it on God's terms.

"The Lord God took the man and put him in the garden of Eden to till it and keep it . . . then the Lord God said, 'It is not good that the man should be alone; I will make him a helper fit for him . . . and they [shall] become one flesh' " (Genesis 2:18-24).

Suggested Activity for Chapter 11

1. It has been said that people marry today with expectations higher than those of their grandparents several generations ago. List what you think your great-grandparents expected of their marriage. Compare that with what most people expect today.

2. Do you believe the media has led couples today to look at marriage more romantically than realistically? Leaf through several current

magazines noting images portrayed there of children and home life. Discuss what you find.

3. Review again the Genesis story of the creation of man and woman and their loss of the garden as their habitat. Compare their situation to the successes and failures of marriages you have observed.

CHAPTER *12*

The Hub of
the Marriage Wheel

When a couple comes into my office with a marital problem, the first thing I observe is how they communicate. What is the communication style of each partner? Do these styles conflict? Are the partners able to express themselves clearly and effectively? Does each show respect for the other while communicating? How well does each one listen to the other? Is there any attempt to negotiate, or is each trying to win a point? Communication is the hub around which the marriage wheel turns or fails to turn.

We learn to communicate early in life. We observe our parents and model our communication after their methods and manners. Before marriage, each person has thousands of interpersonal confrontations in which he or she learns and practices the type of communication that will take shape in a marital relationship and with one's children. Chapter 8 included a discussion of the great number of decisions that have to be made in the first year of marriage—decisions that have never been made before. All of these decisions must be made through a communication process. Some of the couples I interviewed in my study said they communicated so well that these decisions did not seem difficult. Others develop serious problems in their relationships from the start because of poor communication. The following are two examples of communication which I have observed taking place between marriage partners.

Alice and Lee have had a stormy marriage, and the reason seems to be their lack of ability to communicate with each other. Each, to some degree, is lacking in communcation skills, and practices different communication styles. Let us analyze the problem that Alice and Lee are having. First, there is a temperamental difference. Lee tends to be aggressive, while Alice is defensive. Lee enjoys talking at great length while Alice doesn't like to get involved in long conversations. Alice makes hasty decisions. She can decide very quickly what she thinks about a matter. She dislikes turning a subject over and over and looking at all angles. Once she makes up her mind, that finishes the matter. She doesn't want to review everything after she has made her decision. When something comes to her mind, she wants to talk about it right away, even if Lee is engrossed in watching his favorite television program or reading a book. Alice is very bright, and most of the time her judgment is sound. She says she relies on her feminine intuition.

To Lee, Alice seems blunt and abrupt. Lee enjoys long discussions, even on controversial subjects. Alice avoids controversy whenever possible, saying she gets upset when trying to discuss such subjects with Lee. Lee's style is to analyze a matter, consider each part, and look at all sides. Even if he agrees with Alice, he wants to examine alternatives. Alice is impatient with this and sometimes interprets it as a rejection of her. She lacks a feeling of security and needs a great deal of encouragement and reinforcement. Neither seems to understand the communicative style of the other, and this leads to a great amount of frustration. Lee accuses Alice of being inconsistent and impulsive. Alice says that Lee is impatient and doesn't understand her. When they begin to discuss anything at all, it soon seems to develop into frustration, hurt feelings, misunderstandings, and anger. Lee and Alice are respected and liked by their friends and are active participants in their church and community. Their marriage lacks one thing above all else: they have never learned to communicate with each other.

Let us look at another couple who are able to communicate quite well and throughout their married life have solved problems, managed conflict, and made decisions in a satisfactory manner. The following is their account of one of their discussions about a problem on which they had a difference of opinion.

Tim: I think it is time to plant our vegetable garden.

Judith: I guess so, but I would so much rather use our space for flowers.

Tim: Flowers are nice, but a vegetable garden gives us something to eat. It's so much better than what we can buy in the supermarket.

Judith: True, but don't you agree that something beautiful is just as valuable?

Tim: I appreciate beauty, but I think a plant full of ripe, red tomatoes is beautiful.

Judith: Of course they are beautiful, but I need flowers to look at every day.

Tim: Is there any reason why we can't have both? I may not have as many vegetables as I want; and you won't have as many flowers.

Judith: In that case, we will have to draw a plan of our patio and decide just what goes where.

Tim: I hope we won't have any major problem about that.

Judith: We'll work it out.

Tim and Judith have a lot going for them. They are temperamentally suited for each other. They have much in common, which means their differences are never great. They learned to communicate before they were married. They have studied principles and methods of communication since they were married. Rigidity and defensiveness, which block communication for a great many people, are not a part of their personal characteristics. Their communication vignette indicates that they have respect for each other, are polite, listen to what the other is saying, and are willing to compromise. They are not easily angered or upset. They try to be rational, and even when they are not, they are able to recover, reconcile, and reach a decision with which each can live. Their "communication hub" turns smoothly, and their marriage "wheel" keeps rolling along.

At this point it might be well to consider some of the basic principles of communication: what it is and how it works. Most forms of communication can be classified under two headings: audible and non-audible. If you asked the average person how communication takes place, the answer would probably be by speaking and by using words. This answer would be partly right. Language was invented to help people give information to other people, and language consists of words.

Words are like creatures—they are alive. Each word has a face, a personality, an ancestry, an expression of hope or despair, joy or sorrow, and a life of its own. The word *love* has warmth, stirs up memories out of the past, and stimulates expectations for the future. The word *joy* has a ring to it, calling us to an experience of fun or exhilaration. The word *grandeur* invites us to see beauty, to stand before the mountains and the sea in awe. The word *hate* is vitriolic and stirs up images of violence and evil. A word like *yes* opens gates, invites friendships, and allows love to flourish. The word *no* closes doors, changes courses of action, sends people away, and makes it necessary to reconsider or start over again.

Words begin in the mind. Strange, quivering impulses in the brain take shape and come out as sounds and signals. Within our heads there is this continuous monologue which continues throughout our lives. This silent language emerges into words of various kinds which we must choose and arrange in order to be understood. This is how language came into being, and there are hundreds of different languages in the world. Most of us have a number of words which we can use called our vocabulary. When we want to communicate with another person, we must choose the appropriate words to express what we want to say and reject the ones that might confuse the listener or cause the listener to misunderstand or become angry.

When young people marry, they should become aware of the importance of using certain words that work like magic in a marriage, such as "I love you." This is not said enough after marriage. One of my clients said to me, "Why do I have to tell my wife I love her so often? She knows I do." Does she? Maybe she does, but she still likes to hear it said all her life. Words that are most difficult to say are "I'm sorry," "I was wrong," "Forgive me." There are hurting words and healing words. Omit the hurting words and use the healing words. There are discouraging words and encouraging words, and it makes a great difference which you use. Perhaps you have heard of the *I* messages and the *You* messages. If your partner is always late, you might say, "*You* should be more prompt." Or you could say, "*I* would appreciate it very much if both of us could arrange to be on time. Could we?" I am sure you see the difference in those two ways of using words. All communication should have within it an expression of love, understanding, and compassion.

The closing verse of Psalm 19 reminds us of our proper attitude in communicating: "Let the words of my mouth and the meditation of my heart be acceptable in thy sight, O Lord, my rock and my redeemer." The "meditation of my heart" is where all speech originates. If there is loving-kindness in my heart, it will determine what I say. According to the "words of my mouth," the listener will determine what I mean. If we keep in mind that these words should also be acceptable "in thy sight, O Lord, my rock and my redeemer," then we can be sure that they will be healing words to the one to whom we are speaking.

There are ways other than words that audibly carry our messages to our listeners, such as laughing, crying, sighing, groaning, moaning, humming, gasping, clicking the tongue, whistling, clapping hands, slapping one's side, stomping one's feet, snapping fingers, pounding the table—none of which uses words. We can also use wordless sounds such as *uh-uh, ooo, ahhh*, and so forth. There are also vocal qualifiers. One can speak loudly or softly, angrily or lovingly, in whispers or in shouts, in moderate tones, or by screaming and yelling. Some experts in the field of communication believe that vocal qualifiers are more important than the words themselves. As an exercise, try saying, *"Yes"* and making it mean, "I'm not sure," or even, "No." Then say, *"no"* and make it mean, "Maybe," or even, "Yes." You will begin to see the importance of tonal quality.

There are also the nonaudible forms of communication. You can't hear these, but you can see and interpret them. When people communicate with you, the chances are you will be looking at them. You will notice their facial expressions, the position of their bodies, and the movement of their arms and legs. Are they smiling, frowning, looking at you or away from you, sitting with legs or arms crossed, hands clenched or open? Are they farther from you than seems natural? Are they unusually close to you? Do they touch you occasionally as they talk? All these things mean something to your interpretation of their messages.

Sometimes in seminars for marriage enrichment I have couples practice these different forms of body language. It helps make people conscious of the importance of certain forms of communication that are often not recognized or neglected.

One of the couples in my marriage project shared with me their habit of leaving little notes around the house telling the other of their love and appreciation for what the other did. Some of the couples make a habit of bringing home gifts for the other, particularly if one has been on an out-of-town trip. Writing seems to be a lost art for a great many people, but letters still say a lot that one cannot express verbally to another person. Writing is a very effective form of communication.

Your appearance also speaks for you. From the beginning of your marriage, decide to make a neat, fresh appearance at the breakfast table. The way you look may help in determining the climate for the whole day. My wife and I always took notice of an elderly husband in his eighties who always appeared neat and clean, well-dressed, hair carefully groomed, shoes shined—almost as if he were expecting visitors every day. This said something to us about what he was saying about his self-esteem and his respect for his wife and others.

Several years ago, I participated in a conference in which one of the seminars was titled "The Art of Listening." At first, I was surprised that a seminar could devote its entire time to this subject, but it proved to be very popular and helpful. Perhaps listening is a form of communication that is done most poorly, and married people need to develop their listening skills more fully. Try to become a creative listener who is always asking, "What is this person trying to say to me?" Try responding by saying, "Is this what you are trying to tell me?" and then repeat the message as you received it. Be patient. Give the other person enough time to say what needs to be said. Don't interrupt. Always be empathic by saying to yourself, "If I were the other person, what would I be trying to express in this message?"

Communication is the means by which we relate to one another. It is more important in marriage relations than anywhere else. Later, I will be discussing its importance in conflict management and in handling anger. For now I am talking primarily about communication as a means of understanding one another and expressing love for each other. Intimacy is vitally important to a marriage and is expressed there more deeply and warmly than in any other place. We communicate love and affection in sexual intercourse and in various moments in the course of the day as well. Some people come from families that did not express their affections openly and may have been cold and distant; these people should give special care to creating a new communication style. In the early years of marriage it is necessary to develop habits of expressing affection through audible and nonaudible means. The words you use and your tonal expressions will help do this. Thoughtful acts will tell the other how you feel. Holding hands, hugging, kissing, fondling, and all forms of touching are important. Someone has suggested that every happily married couple should kiss deeply and warmly four times a day. May I add *at least* four times a day. One can learn to become affectionate. Ashley Montagu stressed this point in his book *Touching*,[1] in which he tells how persons develop a more "pleasant and altruistic" response to relationships with people in cultures where infants are kept in close contact with the bodies of their mothers. Touching and closeness should help marriage partners become more "pleasant and altruistic." The successful marriages that I have studied have within them people who have developed this manner of communicating.

In the following you may find some helpful suggestions to keep in mind while developing your communicating style. These may also help in managing conflict and resolving disagreements and differences in your marriage. When communicating:

1. Be honest and open. Don't be afraid to talk about the real issues. Avoid sidetracking by bringing up other issues that could be dealt with at other times.

2. Ask yourself: "How does my partner feel about this matter?" "How would I feel if I were in his or her situation?"
3. Don't establish a fixed position from which you are unwilling to move. If you become rigid, you are almost sure to become defensive, and this blocks the communicating process.
4. Avoid using highly charged words. Measure what you say carefully. Refrain from put-downs and name-calling. If you engage in such practices, you will find it difficult to disentangle yourself from the mess you have created.
5. Don't hit "below the belt." Consider your partner's level of tolerance in accepting your aggressive tactics. On the other hand, don't wear your "belt" around your neck.
6. Listen to your vocal tones. Your tonal expressions may be more important than your words. Never scream or yell. This can cause severe emotional damage to you and your partner.
7. Consider your "body language." What are your face, hands, arms, and body position saying?
8. Do you have an inclination to run away? Freeze up? Lose control? Any of these may defeat your attempt to communicate constructively.
9. Practice listening. Concentrate on what the other person is saying. Be still for a minute or longer, if necessary, to digest the message or regain your composure. Silence, when used properly, is an effective communicative approach.
10. It may be necessary to attempt to repeat what you think your partner has said, asking, "Is this what you meant?"
11. Say to yourself, "I am not in this to win or to cause my partner to lose. I want to find out what is best for both of us."
12. Remember that in a great many instances, negotiating is the way to go. This involves giving and taking. Consider alternatives and compromises.
13. Agree to disagree if necessary. Say, "Maybe we can't find the solution now, but let's think it over and come back to it later."
14. If you become angry, admit it. Say, "I'm angry about this, but I don't want to be angry with you. I love you. Let's talk it out and get to something positive."
15. If your communication becomes heated and intense, say, "I love this person, and though we are differing and hold some strong convictions about our positions, I am going to show love and understanding."
16. Practice communicating while holding hands. Touch more often in

the course of the day. It will say something more than words can say.

17. Be patient. Remember that your goal is to solve problems, make good decisions, and find happiness for both you and your spouse through effective relating.
18. Think of communicating as an art and yourself as a developing artist.

Communication is the hub around which the marriage wheel turns. It is at the center of almost everything that happens in your days together. If the hub breaks down, everything goes with it. If it is sound and working, everything is more likely to move toward a bright future.

Communication comes from the heart. Let your prayer be in the words of the psalmist:

"Let the words of my mouth, and the meditation of my heart, be acceptable in thy sight, O Lord, my rock and my redeemer."

Suggested Activity for Chapter 12

1. Use the suggestions at the end of the chapter to analyze your communication style. Ask someone who knows you intimately to comment on how he or she sees you as a communicator.
2. Make a list of ways in which you hope to improve your methods of communicating.
3. Read Psalm 19, concentrating on verse 14. How would you describe meditations "of the heart"? In what way is your communication style related to your inner spiritual nature?

CHAPTER 13

It Takes Two to Tangle

My wife, Janet, tells me that one of the adjustments she had to make when she married me was the transition from living with one person, herself, to living with two—from a single to a double occupancy. Who can deny that marriage is one of the greatest experiences in life and one which calls for major changes and adjustments? Here one enters an environment which brings about a closeness and intimacy that is experienced nowhere else. It is not only joyful but stressful. The joy comes from having a partner to double your pleasures and halve your sorrows. The stress comes from facing the challenges, the crises, the problems, the conflicts, and frustrations that marriage brings to everyone.

A young wife wrote to me, "It isn't simple for one person to learn how to live this life, and to think we put two together and expect them to make it in a marriage!" All of us know of the conflicts we have within ourselves. What about adding another person to complicate matters! In dancing it "takes two to tango." There's no fun dancing the tango with oneself—in fact, it is impossible. The marriage dance, as we have seen, can be full of harmony and joy. It also takes two to tangle, and two often do. This doesn't mean "tangling" is detrimental to a relationship. In fact, it can strengthen it.

Much has been written on this subject in recent years. Perhaps the greatest publicity came in a book entitled *The Intimate Enemy* by Bach and Wyden.[1] I never liked thinking of my wife as an "enemy"—even a friendly one. Though the authors speak of spouses as "intimate enemies" who are "fighting" one another, they are careful in defining the nature of the fighting and the rules under which the fighting is to take place. Other therapists recommend aggressive fighting as therapeutic. Though this may be helpful to some, I have never used it in my practice. I would not define the process by which conflicts are resolved as a fight. It is a confrontation between two people who disagree and who may do so with considerable intensity.

Many couples beginning married life do not expect to have conflicts. In fact, some go to great lengths to avoid them. To these people I would say that all good marriages experience conflict because all partners run into differences which must be met and resolved. Do not be afraid to face your differences and disagreements. Working through them can be healthy exercise in making the marriage grow and become more resilient.

In my study of successful marriages, I discovered that all the couples in the project had problems and disagreements not totally different from those in failing marriages. The difference was that they knew how to work through these problems and disagreements. No couple, no matter how promising their prospects, are completely compatible. There will be some differences. It was Ogden Nash who described marriage as "a legal and religious alliance—entered into by a man who can't sleep with the window shut and a woman who can't sleep with the window open."

Differences can add zest to a marriage when accepted in good spirits. Janet's father and mother were at opposite ends of the pole politically. Her father was a staunch Republican, and her mother was a loyal Democrat. During their fifty-three years of married life they often discussed their positions and gave evidence of enjoying doing so. My father was an avid fisherman and checkers player. My mother engaged in neither activity. There were some things my mother enjoyed apart from my father. They were satisfactorily married for sixty-five years.

The couples in my study settled their differences through discussion, as they preferred to label it. They didn't like the term "quarreling," and some objected to the word "argument" to describe their confrontations. I have no objection to that word in its classical sense: "a course of reasoning, or discussion of different points of view."

What are some of the matters that cause conflict in marriages? Again, let us remember the many decisions that couples must make in their first year of marriage. Surely, they are not going to agree on all of them.

I asked the young married people in one of my classes to tell me about difficult areas with which they had to cope in the early years of their marriages. Here are some of their replies:

"Learning to deal with relatives and in-laws."

"How to fight constructively so you accomplish something positive rather than 'garbage dump' and go over old business again and again."

"Working through the nitty-gritty details of sharing the same space, using the bathroom, and deciding who is responsible for carrying out the trash."

"Budgetary problems have to be our major difficulty."

"The learning and putting up with nit-picking habits and routines that have been established for many years in your spouse."

"Sharing enough time with your spouse."

"Learning to like the same kinds of people."

"Trying to relate to your mate and a child at the same time."

"Deciding who cooks, does the laundry, and balances the checkbook."

"Sexual issues—how often, and who initiates?"

"Agreeing on how clean the house should be."

"He liked outdoor living and strenuous activities. I had never gone camping."

"Trying to get enough time to be alone."

"We had different value systems."

On one occasion I counseled a couple who had been married a few weeks. Ned was a contractor and Jeri was a very competent business-woman. Upon being married to Ned, Jeri supposed she would assume an important role in Ned's business. This had never been discussed before marriage—Jeri just took it for granted. She was capable, she thought. She could save Ned's firm money and would enjoy working with him. However, Ned was shocked at the suggestion of such an idea. "I do not want my wife having anything to do with my business," he told her. An argument followed which developed into a bitter quarrel. They separated, came for counseling, but the conflict was never resolved. Later, they divorced. The failure, as I saw it, was in the inability of either of them to negotiate a reasonable compromise. The whole quarrel seemed so unnecessary, perhaps I should say, stupid.

How might we summarize some of the causes of conflict we have noted thus far? The following are not listed in the order of importance or frequency:

1. Money—how to get enough and how to spend it.

2. Sexual relations—what kind, how often, and who initiates?
3. In-laws—what kind of a relationship is beneficial?
4. Division of labor—who does what, when, and where?
5. Privacy—when and how much for each?
6. Manners—in eating, sleeping, cleanliness, talking, etiquette, relating to friends and relatives, dress, and appearance.
7. Making friends—selecting ones agreeable to both.
8. Use of leisure time—doing things together that make for companionship.
9. Use of television, video games and computers—how much time and what type of programs.
10. Children—whether to have or not; if so, how soon and how many? How should they be disciplined?

You may be able to add to the list. There are myriads of circumstances, any one of which could be a cause for conflict. Yet, any of these has a good chance of being resolved by the skill called "negotiation." Negotiation is that facet of communication in which two people engage in a process of give and take until a satisfactory solution is reached. I will try to discuss in some detail how one can develop the skill that is needed in this process.

First, however, let us consider the attitudes and temperamental characteristics that are needed to facilitate the process. The "sweet-tempered" people are more adept at negotiating than those who are irritable, sullen, and hot-tempered. Defensiveness is a block in this process. Resolve to shed your defensive armor—you don't need it. Be honest, empathic, and open, willing to listen and compromise. Also, enter marriage believing that both of you are equal in value and importance. Conflict resolution by means of one spouse dominating the other is no resolution. With that as a background, let us examine one of the methods used in a training program in problem solving and conflict management. This method was conducted by a team under the direction of Carl Ridley of the Division of Child Development and Family Relations at the University of Arizona.[2]

Twenty-six couples participated in an eight-week, 24-hour problem-solving training program, while 28 similar couples participated in an eight-week, 24-hour relationship discussion group. The former group was trained to use a process for solving problems, while the latter group merely discussed interpersonal relationships. All of the participants ranged in age from 18 to 24. All were anticipating marriage. Results indicated that the problem-solving group that received specific training, as compared to the relationship discussion group without the training, showed a significant increase in communication and mutual problem-solving skills. This indicates a difference between talking about problem solving and engaging in a training program in which a couple practices the skill. It has been my philosophy for years, in working with couples both before and after marriage, to do more than discuss relationships. I want couples to learn to relate by practicing the art of relating. By doing this, they are much more apt to retain the skill later in the marital relationship as it works itself out day by day. If you are contemplating marriage or are already married and feel you need more skill in problem solving, enter a workshop where you can receive training.

In the program supervised by Ridley and associates, each couple began by facing each other and engaging in practicing three communication skills: owning thoughts and feelings, listening and reflecting thoughts and feelings, and using open and closed questions. Partners took turns speaking and listening about issues they were trying to understand and solve.

In order to help you understand and experience this process, I am suggesting you ask your partner to join with you in each step of the program as it was carried out in the original study. First, select a problem that might be relevant to your particular situation. If necessary, refer to those suggested in the list noted earlier in this chapter.

Step 1. Explore the problem. Each should talk about the issue until both understand the nature of the problem and its effect on them.

Step 2. Define the problem in relationship terms. Ask, "Does this affect one or both of us? How important is it to reach a solution? Do we both agree to work together toward a solution?"

Step 3. Identify how each partner contributes to the problem. This step is for the purpose of showing that rarely is one member the sole cause of the problem. Each should ask and answer: "What did I do to cause this problem?" By the end of Step 3, each partner should have a better understanding of the nature of the problem and how each feels about it.

Step 4. State a goal that you desire to attain in ways of relating to each other—what behavior patterns need to be increased, decreased, or changed? Each asks and the other answers: "Do I have any manner of communicating with you that you particularly like or dislike?"

Step 5. Suggest alternative solutions. Brainstorm, making a list of all the possible solutions each can generate. Write them down for consideration in the next step.

Step 6. Discuss each suggested solution to see if it would achieve the desired goal, solve the problem, and be consistent with each partner's values and resources.

Step 7. Select the one solution both partners think is best for them. Decide which role each person should play in carrying it out.

Step 8. Begin the process of implementing this particular way of solving the problem. Set a time period in which the process is to be tested.

Step 9. Evaluate your progress. This involves partners discussing and evaluating what was accomplished over several days or weeks.

If you carried out each step together, what was the result? Do you feel that you better understand the process by which problems are solved and conflicts are resolved? To some, this process may seem to be mechanical, academic, or at best, attempting to role-play real-life situations. Even if it does, there is value in following this process—it is compatible with any learning procedure.

I remember how I learned to play golf. I read magazines and books describing how to swing the club and strike the ball. I could have read for months or years, but that alone would never make me a golfer. The next step I needed to take was to go out with an instructor and watch him demonstrate the near-perfect swing and hit. Now I could visualize the way to do it, but I still couldn't play golf. Next, the instructor put the club into my hands and said, "Now, let's see you do it." He was patient with my clumsy efforts as I "whiffed" the ball several times. When I did manage to hit it, I couldn't get it in the air. Reminding me of a few fundamentals, he left me to practice. At the next lesson he continued to watch my efforts to hit the ball, making occasional suggestions. After years of practice and playing the game, I am still no expert, but I do have some skill that makes it possible for me to enjoy the game.

If learning to play a game for recreational purposes takes all of that training and practice, what would make anyone think he or she could step into the important "game" of marriage and possess the all-important skills of problem solving and conflict management without training? To succeed in marriage is infinitely more important than to become proficient in a sport such as golf, tennis, or racquetball. Yet thousands of couples enter marriage as rank amateurs and think they will, in some way, fumble their way through to competency.

Bob and Karen are a couple in my study of successful marriages. They have attended training sessions in problem solving and conflict management. Although they have achieved considerable skill in this area, they still continue to work at it. In one interview I had with them, some of the steps in the program we have just considered are illustrated.[3]

Karen: It's your basic attitude that makes the difference. First we say, "Let's work on it," and secondly, we know we can find a solution.

We go at it knowing we have the ability, the skills, and the attitude to help us find a solution.

J.R.H.: Why don't you get upset?

Karen: Oh, we do. And sometimes we get angry, too. But we don't get loud or scream and yell. That's not our style. But we let each other know how we think and feel. If things are real tense, if at all possible, we stick with it until we feel comfortable in leaving each other.

Bob: We have hurt each other, but for the most part, we think there are better strategies. We had a round last night that got pretty thick. We stuck with it until we found some resolutions. And even though we were very angry, our overall positive regard and friendship for each other were not diminished or threatened by this.

J.R.H.: How did you do this? What was the process?

Karen: The very first step is to get the matter out on the table. And that for me is the most important matter. As a child I was not allowed to show anger. So, I had to learn how to express anger constructively. This is one of the growing areas of my life in which I have done a lot of work. I now know how to express my feelings constructively rather than that 'below the belt' kind of thing. It still takes me awhile to get it out on the table. I start out being very rational and diplomatic. It takes a little while before I can open up the gate and let it out.

Bob: The second step is what we tried to do last night. We tried to discover what all the issues in our conflict were and bring them together into one. Then we went back and forth until we found a resolution.

Karen: Lately we have been working on some skills to help us do this. It helps you to know how to solve your problems. I have a better understanding now about how Bob will react under certain situations when I say or do something, and by asking him to tell me how he feels, I am helped to understand. This way, I am more able to deal with Bob where he's really at, rather than on some ethereal plain.

J.R.H.: Do you have confidence now after thirteen years of marriage that you can meet any problem or conflict successfully?

Bob: Yes, we do.

Here is an example of a couple who have the important combination of spirit, attitude, and method. And it is interesting that couples who have had training in and have given the matter of problem solving considerable thought find they are following a plan in real-life situations. I am told that after several years of practicing the game of golf, the player develops a "built-in" swing that operates almost without thought. Perhaps in marriage, couples can develop a "built-in" communication rhythm that will help them solve their problems and resolve their conflicts.

There is another important matter which must be mentioned in relation to "tangling" and resolving conflicts, and that is the phenomenon of anger. According to David Mace, processing anger is one of the most important matters in improving marriage relationships.[4] What is anger and how does it come about? The anticipation of something unpleasant, threatening, annoying, perplexing, or demanding can trigger stress reactions causing fear or anger. Traditionally, anger has been explained as nature preparing us for a fight, flight, or freeze. It is possible for anger to be transmitted to the appropriate region of the brain without much chance of its being processed by our rational faculties. Although the capacity to become angry is possessed by everyone, each person reacts differently to anger stimuli. Most married couples notice this difference.

Anger may be a part of nature's survival kit. However, love and common sense determine what to do with your anger. They ask such questions as, "How can anger be used creatively in our relationships? What do we wish to accomplish?" The apostle Paul advises, "Be angry, but do not sin; do not let the sun go down on your anger" (Ephesians 4:26). I would interpret this to mean that though you may be angry, do not allow yourself to engage in angry, hurtful, sinful acts, thus letting your anger get out of control and cause damage to a relationship. Then he adds this very helpful note—don't let the day pass without working through your anger and resolving it. Many of the couples in my study of successful marriages have told me they never let anger or bad feelings go unattended before they go to bed at night.

What are some of the basic principles that will help us in dealing with "anger before sundown" and bring positive results to a marital relationship? Consider the following:

1. Let us accept the fact that even though two people love each other very much, there will be times when each will become angry. One hopes that as time goes by, the anger episodes will diminish into milder forms of expression.

2. When one becomes angry, it is best to acknowledge the fact. Remember, when you first feel an emotion coming on, it is not clearly defined. Is it fear, hostility, anger, or what? It may come upon you as a result of losing an argument; feeling frustrated; resisting change; or experiencing a sense of insecurity, unworthiness, or powerlessness. By talking about it, you can allow your mind to take over and begin to intellectualize the situation. You are now helped to break an otherwise

vicious chain of reactions that could accelerate to a point where it could cause serious damage. Now you are more able to cope with the situation; your spouse will know what's going on inside of you and will be more able to work with you in arriving at a solution.

3. There is another approach which I try to practice and try to teach any client who comes to me with an anger problem. It might be called "reflective responding." When someone says something or acts in a way that tends to anger you, reflect on why he or she does so. Maybe he is ill or has had a difficult day; maybe she has been annoyed by someone else or is suffering from indigestion or a headache. Reflective responding will help us deal with anger by first helping us to consider what might be the cause of the provocation. The age-old advice of counting to ten before speaking in anger is still valid. It gives one time for reflection. It works in maintaining good relationships in a marriage.

4. The next step comes from remembering that love is the most important characteristic of the relationship between you and your spouse. So it helps you say, "I don't want to be angry with you, but I need to understand what is wrong and work through it. Will you help me? We need to work on this together since we are both involved." By this time angry feelings should have subsided and both partners should be able to discuss the problem more rationally. It is now seen not as a problem of one or the other but one for which both must assume responsibility and process together. Reconciliation and a return of good feelings are much more possible by this time.

By way of summary, let us agree that problems, disagreements, conflicts, angry feelings, and heated confrontations are common to all marriages. No one should be afraid of them. They are opportunities for growth and development. They, in themselves, can never destroy a marriage. It is the ability or the inability to cope with them that matters. This takes skill, a positive attitude, and a great amount of love. The process consists of bringing the problems out into the open, examining them thoroughly, accepting the fact that both partners are involved, exploring solutions, and working together to bring about what is best for both.

In all your "tangles" remember you are committed to a love relationship, and even in the midst of a disagreement your spouse is your "intimate friend." Harry Stack Sullivan put it in a way that has become a classical definition of the goal of marriage: "When the satisfaction or the security of another person becomes as significant to one as is one's own satisfaction or security, then the state of love exists."[5]

What we are discussing here is how to find a way to carry out what Apostle Paul has asked us to do:

"Let all bitterness and wrath and anger and clamor and slander be put away from you, with all malice, and be kind to one another, tenderhearted, forgiving one another, as God in Christ forgave you" (Ephesians 4:31).

Suggested Activity for Chapter 13

1. If you are engaged or already married, make a list of the areas in which you are most likely to have disagreements with your partner. Why do you think you disagree? What compromises have you suggested or tried?
2. Choose an area of disagreement with your spouse and try using the nine steps suggested in this chapter to make progress in dealing with it. What happened?
3. Make a list of circumstances that cause you to be angry. What do you do when you realize you are angry?
4. Read Matthew 5:23-24. What does reconciliation with an important person in your life have to do with your relationship with God? How does reconciliation happen?

Section III
Where the Harvest Begins

CHAPTER *14*

Where Your Treasure Is

Patty married Hal believing they were compatible. What she didn't know about was his passion for sport cars. She soon found out. Hal came home one day announcing he had just located the car he had always dreamed about. "But we can't afford it. We have no money," Patty warned. "Oh, but Patty," replied Hal, "you don't know what this means to me. I can't live without it." Hal's love of sport cars was but one of the illustrations of the difference between the two. Patty came from a family devoted to art, literature, and music. All her family were loyal church members. Hal's family was quite the opposite, with little interest in any of these areas. In other words, their treasures were in two different places. Patty and Hal felt they were in love, and that justified their marriage. They had not stopped to consider what eventually proved to be an insurmountable barrier.

Many years ago, social psychologist E.G. Williamson made a profound statement about this matter: "I believe behavior of all types originates in value commitments, and frequently in conflict and confusion about value motivation."[1] This seems to me to be a commentary on what Jesus said: "For where your treasure is, there will your heart be also" (Matthew 6:21). "Your treasure," your valuables—are the source of your life—"your heart."

The word "heart" in this passage might be translated in a modern sociological term as "lifestyle." One's lifestyle is recognized in one's behavior. I know you by observing what you do: your actions, your language, how you treat me, and how you treat others. I can observe your habits, your manners, your relationships, and your conduct throughout the day. When you meet another person, you react according to how that person relates to you. You come to love and want to marry someone by this same route. Our judgments are made by what we see. I cannot read your thoughts or explore your motives. I *can* observe what you do. This may be misleading, particularly in the dating and courtship period. For a limited period of time people are able to regulate their behavior in order to please another. Patty didn't know the real Hal before marriage. He had been very thoughtful and attentive. After marriage, however, people generally reveal their true selves within a short period of time, as Hal did. Marriage quickly uncovers the place where our treasure is hidden.

Though observable behavior is important, the source of behavior is still more important—"where your treasure is, there will your heart be also." This means having a more in-depth knowledge of the person you want to live with the rest of your life. What implication does this have for people preparing for or who are in the early years of marriage? Consider the fact that compatibility depends to a great extent on the value systems of the two partners. This matter has become increasingly important to family life educators and marriage counselors in recent times. If E.G. Williams is right, then "behavior of all types originates in value commitments." How we behave, how we relate in marriage, depends on the values to which we are committed. If two people are committed to the same values, there is reason to believe they will get along much better than otherwise.

What are values and how do they affect behavior? Philosophers have chosen beauty, truth, and goodness as the ultimate values. These cover a vast number of things people cherish in their life experiences. Abraham Maslow prepared what became his famous hierarchy of needs, which at the base had the primary values: food, shelter, and safety. Higher on the pyramid were relationship needs: to be given love, warmth, and affection by another person. On the next level were the needs for the respect and esteem of others. On the highest level was the need for self-realization—being able to achieve, to accomplish something worthwhile, and to be recognized by one's peers as being successful. Needs and values are closely related in that one tends to value what he or she feels is needed for personal fulfillment.

When people were asked in a public opinion poll what they wanted in life, most replied that they wanted "love." I have surveyed the needs of married couples in my study and found that they run true to form. A basic need is for security found in a partnership and a home. This involves an adequate income to give a couple a satisfactory standard of living. While it is true that "Man shall not live by bread alone" (Matthew 4:4), without bread he cannot begin to live. My studies also show that loyalty, responsibility, and unselfishness are considered very valuable to a marriage. Then there are values that determine our cultural pursuits: art, literature, crafts, music, and travel. I have found it interesting to have couples check lists indicating what kinds of books and magazines they read, what music they prefer, what kinds of television programs they would choose—all of which are indicators of value systems. Food is an important value for some, a lesser value for others. Lynn is a gourmet cook. She spends long hours studying gourmet magazines, preparing special recipes, putting together intricate sauces, and fashioning delicate desserts. Tad, the man who wishes to marry her, would prefer an ordinary meal of meat, potatoes, and apple pie. How will Lynn react to his "treasures" on the dinner plate?

I remember neighbors whose household reflected two different value systems related to organization and neatness. Mrs. W. was a meticulous housekeeper. Everything had to be immaculately clean and in its place. The living room was never used except for company. Mr. W. was careless in dress and in habits. He spent most of his time in the kitchen and garage. For Mrs. W., neatness, cleanliness, and organization were values she cherished very highly. Her husband couldn't have cared less for these values. Can you imagine the tension in that household? Values touch every aspect of our lives. "Everything we do, every decision we make and course of action we take, is based on our consciously or unconsciously held beliefs, attitudes, and values."[2]

A marital therapist friend of mine puts so much importance on value compatibility in a marriage that he uses as his main instrument an inventory that indicates the operating values in a marital relationship. He believes values are clues to whether a couple is functioning well together or having excessive conflicts. He asks couples to rate themselves as to where they are now, where they were at the time they were married, and where they would like to be in the future. The areas in which couples rate their relationship are religion, hobbies, money, children, communication, meals, sex, habits, continuing education, recreation, time together, friends, and television viewing. He says that it soon becomes apparent that individuals differ from one another in their values and that they regard the expression of their values as important sources of satisfaction and happiness.

John and Nancy came to him for help. After reviewing their work on his inventory, he concluded that they seemed to have developed their value systems as legacies from their parents and rigidly refused to change them. Early in life, Nancy learned to believe that good little girls were submissive and obeyed their parents; and good wives pleased and obeyed their husbands. Wives and mothers could only attain happiness by sacrificing themselves for husband and family. John grew up modeling himself after his father, a strong, hard-working, serious man who seldom showed affection, and flew into rages over matters which annoyed him. John's father thought of himself as undisputed boss in the family. John adopted his father's values and beliefs when he had a family of his own. Nancy's values of loyalty and respect made it possible to live with John, but with increasing resentment. John and Nancy had two problems: conflicting value systems and lack of skill in resolving value conflicts.

It must be noted that values are often associated with highly charged emotional states. John believed strongly in the value of being the boss, whose word was final in his family. Anyone disputing this fact would be the object of John's wrath.

Most of us will defend our values with conviction and emotional vigor. This is particularly true when it comes to our moral values—what we believe is right and what is wrong. Annette was severely shocked when she was called by the police and told that her husband, a very respectable man in the community, was caught shoplifting. She was shattered emotionally, trying to reconcile her value system of honesty and integrity with her husband's action. Moral and ethical values play an important role in people's lives.

The couples in my successful marriage study emphasized the importance of their agreement on religious beliefs and practices. They felt their religious values determined much of their philosophy of life, their interests, their activities, and vocational aspirations. Norm and Doris are officers in their church, teachers in the church school, and among its leading supporters. Norm said, "I think our adjustment in marriage was due in part to our similar religious backgrounds." Said Doris: "It has affected our whole value system, and since we are such busy people, going to church is one of the few things we do together as a family." Their enthusiasm for what their church can mean in their lives and in the life of their community has spread to their children who will carry on these family traditions. There is no doubt about it—values play an important role in the lives of people, and doubly so in the relationships between two people in marriage. "Where your treasure is, there will your heart be also." And hearts need to be united.

This leads us to inquire, "From whence do values come? What is their origin?" It is my contention that they come from our basic beliefs. Is it not true that the fountainhead of all values emerges from what one believes about God, the meaning of human beings, and the purpose of life? The great questions of the ages are: Who am I? What am I here for? What is my destiny? Are we at the mercy of the "trampling march of unconscious power" (one philosopher's way of talking about the crushing power of blind chance), or are we in the hands of a loving Being? Are we here as a result of the forces of chance or purpose? As we answer these questions, so shall we live. Gerhard Lenski made a study of religion and family life and concluded in his book, *The Religious Factor*,[3] that according to the particular socio-religious group to which a person belongs, there would be a marked difference in his or her attitude toward job, buying habits, national goals, politics, sociological views, attitudes toward race, family values, education, and many other areas.

Henry and Doris, a couple in my marriage study, have had more than fifty years of happiness together. To hear them talk about their enduring relationship is to be inspired. In one of my interviews with them I asked for the secret of their successful marriage. Henry replied that they were both raised in Christian homes and taught Christian beliefs, which have sustained them all through their lives. Henry concluded with, "Do you know anyone who would want to live in a community without a church?" That was a thought-provoking question, wasn't it? What is there in the life of a community or a nation that is valuable that is not related to what someone believed with sincere conviction? Many who would not acknowledge their debt to those who brought Judeo-Christian beliefs to this nation are, nevertheless, warming their hands over the religious hearth fires of the past, which have given us our democratic and human values.

When I read the New Testament, I am reminded that the Gospel, the Good News, is that God is love and in Jesus God is telling us that the divine purpose is to bring all God's children together in the power of God's reconciling love. Because of this belief, a couple in marriage can make love and reconciliation their supreme value.

There seems to me to be a progression through all of this. The progression is from beliefs to values to goals. Let me give an example. I believe in the dignity and worth of every person I meet, because that person is a child of God. Because I believe this, the person takes on value, and I treat him or her as valuable. Because I cherish this value, my wife and children take on an added dimension in my life, and I love and respect them in a special way. I begin to see the purpose of my life in loving and relating to others in order to build a community in its truest sense. I know why I am here and where I want to go. I feel that I am cooperating with a divine plan — "thy kingdom come, and thy will be done on earth as it is in heaven" (Matthew 6:10). My values become commitments and lead me toward purposeful goals.

It is necessary for me, from time to time, to review and reinforce my beliefs, to take inventory of my values and value commitments, and to rechart my life course. I recommend this to all couples at the beginning of the married life and throughout that life. It will keep you together and possibly bring you closer as time goes by. For "where your treasure is, there will your heart[s] be also."

Now take inventory of your beliefs, values, and goals by using the following outline.

What Do You Believe?

Partner I	Partner II
1.	1.
2.	2.
3.	3.
4.	4.
5.	5.
6.	6.
7.	7.
8.	8.

What Values Do You Cherish?

1.	1.
2.	2.
3.	3.
4.	4.

5.   5.

6.   6.

7.   7.

8.   8.

What Are Your Life Goals?

1.   1.

2.   2.

3.   3.

4.   4.

5.   5.

6.   6.

7.   7.

8.   8.

Suggested Activity for Chapter 14

1. Fill out the outline at the end of this chapter in which you and your partner will list your beliefs, values, and goals. Compare and discuss. To what extent are they compatible? Where is additional work needed?
2. Select one of your important religious beliefs and trace its progression in helping you formulate your values and goals.
3. List the values that are taught in the Christian faith as found in the New Testament. How do they affect personal living, human relationships, and a concept of life purpose?

CHAPTER *15*

And Baby Makes Three

It has been a long time since our first child arrived on the scene, but I remember the details very clearly, more so than the arrival of our second or third child. This will not be a chapter on all the details of pregnancy, childbirth, and the nurture of the first child. All that information is available to you in an abundance of current literature on those subjects. I will devote these pages to some of the basics concerning the transition from a two-person family to a three-person family, as I remember the experience and have learned from it.

I am inclined to believe that getting married was the number one life-changing event in my life and having our first child was number two. They both brought about dramatic transitions but, at the same time, were very different from each other. Although there are some matters requiring adjustment when a spouse enters your life, there are also many advantages. You now have a partner, a helpmate, who will work with you in making plans, solving problems, and meeting needs. What about the next transition—having your first child? First, there are nine months of pregnancy, and there is nothing a woman has experienced before that is quite like that. Then there is giving birth to your first child, and that is something different from anything that ever happened before. Men also find these experiences to be awesome and traumatic.

Now you have this helpless little infant in your arms. It can't walk!

It can't talk! It can't do anything for itself. It depends entirely on parents for survival. You will have to feed it, bathe it, clothe it, change it, and try to figure out what is wrong when it cries. You will listen to every sound, observe every movement, and wonder what all the sounds and movements mean. Your sleep will be disturbed, your time schedule will be rearranged, and your life will be very different in many ways. Most of us who have had children would not have it otherwise, and we learned to accept it and enjoy it. However, there were many experiences no one told us about. We were not as prepared as we might have been.

There are all sorts of reasons why people have or do not have children. I don't think either choice should be made without careful thought. It is a matter to be considered before a marriage takes place. Important questions should be asked: "Do we like children? Do we want children? If we do, how soon and how many?" The reason these questions should be considered before marriage is that any disagreement on any one of them could cause serious problems after the marriage. If couples agree that they do not want children, then it would be best for them to know this and act accordingly.

Nancy and Bill decided not to have children of their own, even though Nancy says, "I feel that we both think we would be good parents to children growing up. When Jim was growing up, his parents were divorced. During my childhood my parents were fighting constantly. Then after we were married, we had so many things to do that a lot of time has gone by. Bill is 35 and I'm 30. Someday we may adopt, but now Bill has several years in which to complete his medical training, and then a career to think about."

When I counsel a couple such as Bill and Nancy I accept their decision, but I always leave them with this advice: be sure the decision you are making now is the one with which you will be satisfied fifteen or twenty years from now. Then, of course, it will be too late to have children of your own.

Some couples have children for questionable reasons. I have had it said to me, "My parents want us to have children. My mother keeps asking us when we are going to provide a grandchild for them." A couple may feel obligated to fulfill their parents' wishes or to perpetuate the human race. (After all, we are just one generation away from extinction.) So children are brought into the world as the result of a feeling of family or social responsibility. I have known couples who have mistakenly thought that having children would help solve some of their marital problems. Having them only intensified their problems. I suppose some couples want children who will fulfill some of their unrealized dreams and ambitions. ("I want my child to have everything I didn't have!") Some children come as a result of an accident rather than planning. In this case any timing the couple may have had in mind is upset and thrown off course. None of these reasons for having children is sound and such reasons may cause unnecessary difficulty later.

What are good reasons for having children? If one were to ask most couples why they have children, they would say, "Because we like them and want them." And that may be as good a reason as any. This may be the result of a certain kind of social feeling they have for other people, young and old. Janet and I wanted a family to complete our concept of a home. Just the two of us could never have accomplished this for us. Most couples begin with one child. (The chance of having twins in this country is 1 in 84.) Having one child constitutes a family triangle. If a second child is added, you have a family square. And if there are three or more, you have a family circle. If one were to decide which was best for socializing, the family circle might be best, but there are so many considerations that could dictate otherwise. Financial conditions, the physical and emotional health of parents, and various situational factors must be taken into consideration before deciding on the size of your family.

If we hold to the theological concept of the order of creation, then having children is becoming a part of this order. God is a creator, and we are cooperating in God's creative process. In desiring children, we are also recognizing our mortality and attempting to compensate for it. In our children we are extending our life, our faith, and our goals into the future. Our children will carry on in a purposeful way, we hope, after we are gone. Rudolph Dreikurs has written: "A profound feeling for life, a deep interest in the future easily leads to the desire to have children. For through our children we offer mankind something more than we ourselves—the next generation."[1]

Recently I reviewed my family line that began in this country in 1639. I have the names of my direct line of ancestors from then until now. It instills within me a sense of continuity, which I suppose gives me a feeling of immortality by way of a family tree. Here is something that began long ago and is growing. Each child along the way is a part of this intergenerational movement through history.

There was a time when not to have children was a sign of an unfulfilled marriage. I can remember an aunt and uncle who wanted but were not able to have children for certain physiological reasons. When I was still quite young, I felt sorry for them and tried to relate to them as a son might. Today, such a couple's marriage would not seem incomplete to most people. The prevailing attitude is that a couple must know what is best for them.

A secondary consideration in having children today is in being able to support them financially. We are told that the cost of a child from birth through college amounts to a figure between sixty thousand dollars to over one hundred thousand dollars. I would estimate the cost of each child to be between three thousand and six thousand dollars per year, depending on your standard of living and educational expenses. Multiply this by the number of children you expect to have and the rate of inflation, and you will want to plan your family size with care.

Some couples are much better prospects for being parents than others. There are some temperamental characteristics that are important: patience, an even disposition, kindness, persistence, a sense of humor, courage, and joy. Knowledge and training are necessary to fulfill the vocation of being a parent. No one waves a magic wand over us at the birth of our first child, saying, "You can be a good parent now by just doing what comes naturally." For this reason I believe that all prospective parents should attend classes in child nurture and development and read the best books available in this area. I am convinced that most couples are poorly prepared for the responsibility of caring for children. There are so many things I know now that I wish I had known when our first child was born. If couples had to take a test to prove they were knowledgeable in regard to parenting, I wonder how many would pass. Yet is there anything that is more important than being a competent parent?

Another consideration in having children is in being able to offer them a healthy mind and body. To bring a child into the world is an action that requires a profound sense of responsibility on the part of prospective parents. For this child will be living in and affecting life for the next seventy or more years. Most babies are born normal and healthy. However, many are not. In this country between one hundred thousand and one hundred-fifty thousand infants are born each year with congenital malformations, abnormal chromosomes (which cause, for example, Down's syndrome), or a genetic disorder (for example, muscular dystrophy or cystic fibrosis). In the past, birth defects have been attributed to the mother, but recent research suggests that the father is also responsible for certain abnormalities.

In view of this, shouldn't genetic counseling be a part of preparation for having a child? The geneology of each prospective parent can be studied to learn whether they are likely to be carrying genes that could cause defects in a child. Certain blood tests may reveal whether a harmful gene or condition may be present *in utero*. Much advancement has been made in the use of prenatal medicine to insure the health of the child that may otherwise have problems. There are several methods which doctors may use to evaluate the condition of the fetus during pregnancy. One, used particularly for women 35 and older, is known as *amniocentesis*, in which a small amount of amniotic fluid is taken from the mother and analyzed. If there are serious abnormalities indicated, she may decide to have an abortion. (Does a child have a right not to be born?) Such a decision should be made only after consultation with one's husband, a competent physician, and taking into consideration one's religious principles relating to abortion. Or she may decide to continue the pregnancy, preparing for the special needs and care the handicapped child will require. Another technique currently being used is that of *ultrasound*, in which the uterus is scanned with sound waves, thus helping to determine the health of the fetus. Other methods are being developed, but none should be used without the advice of a physician who has expertise in this area of prenatal medicine.

The health of the mother is extremely important previous to and during pregnancy. Good nutrition is essential for the proper growth of the brain cells in the developing fetus. Exercise and invigorating environmental conditions are necessary. Cigarette smoking is hazardous to the health of mother and child. Even the moderate use of alcohol has been demonstrated to be harmful and may cause miscarriages. Drugs are equally harmful, and medication should be taken during pregnancy only on the advice of one's physician.

In view of the fact that there are so many ways of determining whether or not a couple may have a healthy baby and ways of helping them to have a normal child with certain medical and health procedures, it would seem that couples today should give this whole matter of genetic counseling careful consideration.

So, if you can be competent parents in good health, able to provide a home in which love and happiness abide, where children will be welcome and have an opportunity for growth and development, then you have reason enough to plan for your family.

Now, let us take a look at how the arrival of a child affects a marriage. The effect on the new mother may be different from the effect on the new father. Some authorities believe that this is the most unprepared-for role transition in a woman's life. Her physical and emotional life may be affected more intensely at this time than at any other time in her life. Her daily routine is severely altered. When I asked Janet to recall her experience at the time our first child was born, she said among other things, "My life was greatly changed, but it seemed that your life went on very much as usual." This most certainly was true, although today men are more involved in child care than when our first child was born.

It is accurate to say that the arrival of the first child is an interruption in the married life of any couple. This may be a pleasant experience or otherwise, depending on the attitudes of the couple. It must be assumed that life will be different from this point on until the last child leaves home. I have often made the statement that we did not have a full night's sleep for seven years until our last child finished "cutting" teeth. Add to this a hundred things that children do to make life different. And the responsibility for them is always there, day and night. No baby sitter, grandparent, or day-care center can relieve you of this.

E. E. LeMasters,[2] in one of the pioneering studies on the effect of the first child on a marriage (even when the child was wanted), found that in 83 percent of the marriages studied, there was an extensive or severe crisis. The wives admitted to chronic tiredness, confinement to the home, curtailment of socializing, inability to work outside the home, additional responsibilities, and guilt for having these feelings. The fathers felt a decline in sexual response on the part of their wives, new economic pressures, interference with social life, worry about a second pregnancy, and in general, a disenchanted feeling about their own parental role. The entire group that was studied indicated they had completely romanticized parenthood, and they had very little effective preparation for parenthood roles.

A team of students under my direction, desiring to inquire into the effect of children on marriages, sent a questionnaire to 100 couples with children. Sixty-five couples responded, plus 13 individual spouses. (All did not respond to every statement.) Their responses to some of the statements proposed were as follows:

1. Our marriage has improved since we have had children.
    Wives: 52 agreed   12 disagreed
    Husbands: 53 agreed   11 disagreed

2. Our lifestyle changed after our children arrived.
    Wives: 53 agreed   23 disagreed
    Husbands: 56 agreed   8 disagreed

3. Our children have brought us closer together.
    Wives: 47 agreed   19 disagreed
    Husbands: 50 agreed   14 disagreed

4. I feel "tied down" with family matters.

| Wives: | 13 agreed | 59 disagreed |
| Husbands: | 13 agreed | 54 disagreed |

5. Our children have been a disruptive force in our marriage.

| Wives: | 6 agreed | 60 disagreed |
| Husbands: | 8 agreed | 57 disagreed |

6. Our children are "in the way."

| Wives: | 2 agreed | 66 disagreed |
| Husbands: | 4 agreed | 61 disagreed |

7. Our children are our greatest source of pride and joy.

| Wives: | 53 agreed | 13 disagreed |
| Husbands: | 51 agreed | 17 disagreed |

8. We should have remained childless.

| Wives: | 0 agreed | 66 disagreed |
| Husbands: | 1 agreed | 65 disagreed |

9. We come first with each other.

| Wives: | 49 agreed | 17 disagreed |
| Husbands: | 46 agreed | 18 disagreed |

10. Our children have completed our lives.

| Wives: | 56 agreed | 9 disagreed |
| Husbands: | 51 agreed | 15 disagreed |

Their conclusions, for the most part, were that the couples surveyed were very positive about their children and did not consider them to be a disruptive or negative force in their marriages. The students were surprised at their results, having seen other studies showing results running counter to theirs. The couples in my study of competent marriages also have positive feelings about their children and feel that the joy and happiness they have brought far overshadow any inconvenience or disruption. Although some felt their lives changed considerably upon the arrival of the first child, and that meant some degree of disruption, all agreed that the experience was met with great happiness and joy. I have descriptions of this event in the lives of twenty-seven of the spouses in my study, and their statements will speak for themselves.

"It was a planned and happy event! Yes, it brought change in that we are a very gregarious couple and there were new restrictions put on our activities. It was worth every minute."

"While our freedom was curtailed, the birth of our first child brought much joy into our lives. Not only were we thrilled with our first child's birth, but both our parents and friends shared our joy. I, as the mother, did find that it took me close to a year truly to adjust to being at home full time."

"It brought pleasure, a feeling of greater responsibility, and no feeling of disruption."

"Our first child brought joy—now we were a family. I enjoyed immensely the role of being a mother—a sense of accomplishment, and a new closeness in our marriage."

"Joey's birth was a totally joyous occasion. We had wanted a child for quite some time, although I didn't realize how much I would enjoy having a child until after he came. Our lifestyle changed quite a bit, but I seldom if ever think of the pre-child days as happier than after the birth."

"The birth of our first child indeed brought change in living patterns [and] some anxiety, but the joys far outweighed the slight inconveniences and stress."

"I thought our first child was marvelous, beautiful, smart, and exhausting."

I would make an educated guess that when a couple makes a satisfactory adjustment to each other, likes and wants children, and times the arrival of the first child at the most convenient moment, the first child will not be considered a disruptive force and will add to their already beginning state of happiness. On the other hand, when a couple is not satisfactorily adjusted to each other or has excessive problems in the marriage, the arrival of the first child is apt to affect the marital situation adversely.

By way of a summary, I am suggesting some principles for every couple to consider before or when a "baby makes three."

1. Discuss the matters concerning children before you marry. Ask: Do you both like children? How do you relate to children? Do you want children? If so, how many?

2. Prospective mothers and fathers should participate in some kind of training program for parenthood. The husband should participate with his wife in learning about prenatal care and child rearing. Fathers who go through such training will feel closer to their children than fathers who do not. In almost all communities, workshops for parents are available in which people may learn a number of "how-to" skills and share their concerns and anxieties about becoming parents. Take seriously the importance of genetic counseling.

3. Be realistic rather than romantic about what it means to have children. What changes are brought about upon the arrival of a first child?

4. Learn as much as you can about the developmental stages of a child

from infancy through adolescence. Recognize that your child will be temperamentally unique and will not necessarily conform to what other children are being and doing. Developmental time sequences are different for different children. Don't impose unrealistic expectations on your child.

5. Decide to allow several years to pass in your marriage before having your first child. This will give you the important time you need to adjust to each other and get a satisfactory start in your marriage. If there are problems in your marriage, try to work them out before having your first child. Try to have your education completed and some vocational and financial stability before your first child arrives.

6. Resolve never to have an unplanned child. Children need so much to be wanted. Get good contraceptive advice and use it faithfully. This will insure, as much as anything can, the arrival of your children at the time you want them. Your attitude will be entirely different from the attitude you are apt to have with an unplanned child.

7. If you decide to have more than one child, plan your spacing so that the first child and the parents have an adequate start in adjusting before the next one comes along. We felt that a spacing of from 28 to 34 months was about right for us and our children.

8. Try to be good role models for your children. They are great imitators. From the very beginning, what you are will be more effective in their lives than what you say. Students in my classes tell me that their parents' love for each other has been the greatest influence in their lives.

9. Give your child a feeling that he or she is loved and wanted no matter what the circumstances are. Alicerose Barman writes that through facial expressions, vocal tones, and touching and handling the child, we are saying, "You're a very nice baby; we enjoy having you around. We expect you to continue to be a joy, and we'll do all we can to help you." Or you are saying, "You're a nuisance and a pest; life was better without you, and I guess it will only go from bad to worse."[3] Which will it be?

10. Be careful about becoming angry at your child. You will be tired and frustrated many times, but remember this is not a small adult, but a very tiny infant struggling to learn how to survive and grow. In anger, many parents treat their children in a manner they desperately regret after the anger subsides.

11. Do not allow the attention your child is demanding from you to detract from your relationship as husband and wife. This relation-

ship is the first priority in your marriage and all other matters depend on it. Keep your love for each other growing. It is the root system and the main stem of your family plant.

12. Once you become a parent, you will always be a parent. Many things in life can be changed to a "former" status: ex-spouses, ex-jobs, ex-locations, but never ex-children. You will always be these children's mother or father. They will always be your children. This relationship is irrevocable. And it is good for all of us that it is so. Such permanence can bring you lifelong misery or abundant joy, pain or pleasure, grim duty or high privilege—all depending on your attitude and what you make of it. Do not think of your children as problems; think of them as a challenge. Above all, resolve to enjoy them day in and day out.

A friend of mine used to say the future is crawling over the floors of our homes today. The doctors, lawyers, religious leaders, statesmen, teachers, corporation presidents, actors, writers, factory workers, farmers, heads of state, and all the other people of tomorrow are in the cribs, the playpens, the nurseries, and the family rooms of today. Their destinies are in your hands and mine. What an awesome thought! What a responsibility! What a challenge!

When the crowds brought their children to Jesus that he might place his hands on them and pray, the disciples were displeased and asked the people to take their children away. However, Jesus changed all of that: "Let the children come to me, and do not hinder them; for to such belongs the kingdom of heaven" (Matthew 19:14). This is putting a very high value on children, and rightly so. To such belong the kingdoms of tomorrow. What is happening to the children of today in a world of violence, where the nuclear threat hangs over all civilizations, and where stress and tension abound? What is happening to the children of today where families are fractured—leaving two million children each year in situations in this country where parents are separated? Let every couple in the beginning years of their marriage ponder these questions and resolve to be a part of the solution to these problems. Build a healthy, happy marriage for the sake of yourselves and your children. This much you can do.

Suggested Activity for Chapter 15

1. In view of the dangerous population explosion in the world today, what responsibility do parents have to maintain zero population growth by limiting the size of their families?
2. In many instances both husband and wife will be working outside the home at the time their first child is desired. How will pregnancy

and the birth of this child affect the roles and lifestyle of the two? How can this lead to a greater sharing between husband and wife in areas of household duties and child care?

3. To what extent are the gratifications of maternity sufficient to compensate for the reducing of a woman's work outside the home and time spent in non-family interests and social activities? What can be done to increase the contemporary woman's self-esteem in being a mother and devoting herself to family interests?

CHAPTER *16*

Help!
We Can't Do It Alone

I am not thinking only about how we all need help in order to cope with the great crises of life, such as serious illnesses, accidents, financial disaster, death, and similar traumatic events. I am considering the importance of simple support systems to our daily growth and development and how these systems play a part in a couple getting started in married life. Janet and I have been married longer than any other couple in our neighborhood. We have been interested in watching young couples in the process of establishing homes, giving birth to babies, trying to achieve financial stability, climbing the ladder into vocational success, and doing the multitude of things young couples try to do in the course of their early matrimonial journey.

There have been joyful events—weddings, birthdays, family reunions, honors children have received in school, and awards parents have received from the community. There have been sad, even tragic events— a death, a divorce, a fire. The neighborhood mourned the loss of Luke, one of our many dogs, when he was struck by a car. Several burglaries took place in our neighborhood; so we gathered together to discuss how we could help protect one another from such occurrences in the future. When a new family moved in, we gathered together again to welcome them. There is one family that never participates in any attempt to generate a friendly atmosphere. We don't understand this and we are working on it, because we all feel we need one another, even for simple things such as that tall ladder that one family owns, the digging tool we possess, and even that sack of charcoal briquets borrowed because someone forgot to purchase some before company arrived for a cookout.

Living in our neighborhood is somewhat like living in a play, such as Thorton Wilder's *Our Town*, where one participates in the drama of people living with people and people needing people. We can't make it alone! It is as John Donne wrote, "No man is an island, entire of itself; every man is a piece of the continent, a part of the main. . . ."[1] We were not put here for selfish purposes but to help one another, thus fulfilling the law, ". . . love your neighbor as yourself" (Matthew 22:39).

In a discussion group which I was moderating on the subject of meeting crises, a young couple recently married commented, "We haven't had any great crises so far, but frequently we are called on to help other couples." An older man commented, "Just wait awhile, the crises will come; better get ready." Another asked, "What is a crisis, anyway?" What about these three statements?

The word "crisis" comes from the Greek, *krisis*, meaning "turning point." In the case of illness it may mean that crucial time when the patient's condition may worsen or when the patient begins to get well. In a story or drama it is the point at which opposing forces are engaged in the most intensive state of conflict. For most people it represents an event in their lives, often unexpected, that necessitates a sudden and crucial adjustment. In view of the fact that all people have crises, we need to equip ourselves to be helpful to others who are experiencing a crisis, even though we are not.

This kind of helpfulness is a skill and an art. How does one love his neighbor at a time of crisis? It can be put rather simply — put yourself at the disposal of your neighbor. Say, "I know something about what you are experiencing. How can I help?" Take time to listen. Give your neighbor complete freedom in which to ventilate his or her grief or anxiety. Listening is one of the most therapeutic approaches to another's problems. Yet it is one of the most difficult arts to practice. Why is this so? I think it is because we are all too prone to give advice, to say, "If I were you, this is what I would do." However, you are not this other person. Find out what this person thinks the best solution to be, and then encourage and help him or her to carry it through. Walk beside your neighbor as far as you can. The spirit of all this is what is called "empathy." Young couples can be a great source of help to one another. They will find a variety of opportunities in neighborhoods, gatherings of friends, and in church groups. In this sense, we are all called to be a part of the helping professions.

What about the comment of the older man, "Just wait awhile, the crises will come. Better get ready"? Of course, he is right. A friend of ours has multiple sclerosis, and she accepts it and handles it as well as any person we know. She gives helpful talks to groups and titles it "Everyone has an MS." No, it isn't that everyone has what she has. Everyone, she says, has a "miserable something." I have found that to be true in my study of competent marriages. Some people think these happy couples have fewer crises and problems than most. In a study of their crises and how they have met them, I have become convinced that a number of these couples have had more than their share of what some would call "tragedies." One couple found the divorce of their parents to be a serious problem. A wife described a serious automobile accident in which her husband was involved just eleven months after they were married. He suffers permanent pain as a result. Another couple described a serious automobile accident in which two members of the family came close to death. This was followed by brain surgery for the wife and later the birth of a child discovered to be deaf. Another couple described how the husband became infatuated with another woman, which nearly broke up the marriage. They worked through the problem and their marriage is a strong one today. A husband described the long illness of his mother, who finally died of cancer, and the trauma it caused him. Another couple described a rare illness their daughter had at the age of five months that would ordinarily have left the child retarded. A wife told of her plight when she and her husband lived in a foreign country. They had five children when the husband became seriously ill and had to be taken to and kept in a hospital seventy miles away for many weeks. Another couple had a nine-year-old child diagnosed as having a brain tumor. A wife, who participated in active sports, had to have knee surgery, which meant an end to many of the activities she had enjoyed. Another couple related how their son had been beaten severely by an assailant, which resulted in amnesia. Four members in the study experienced the death of their spouses.

Jerry lost her husband when he was in the prime of life. There was no couple in my group of competent marriages, who was a better example of what a loving, devoted couple could be than Jerry and John. She speaks of her experience this way:

"My faith in God hasn't diminished; I still have a strong belief and do still believe that some power other than man sustains this planet. . . . I am very aware now, however, that life is indeed precious and our light can be blown out at any time. I guess I honestly try to live each day as though it might indeed be my last one. I know that for me, the greatest gift that was left to me was the knowledge that I had been completely loved, with no limits or boundaries. That same love has given me courage, strength, and hope for the future."

Jerry's years with John were all too short, but the quality of the love they had for each other was something to behold. It far exceeded a long life where love has faded or disappeared. In her words "life is indeed precious . . . try to live each day as though it might indeed be [the] last one," there is a message for all of us. Even though a couple is in the springtime of their married life, they need to think about how precious each day is and live accordingly. Love as though it were your last chance to love.

I have learned from my couples that in spite of some very serious crises, a marriage can survive and become richer and stronger. How can this be? The reason, I believe, is that these couples have coping power, backed by support systems. Coping power consists of the capacity to say to any crisis, "This has happened to us; we accept it, and we will work through it to bring about the best solution of which we are capable." Coping power consists of courage, strength of character that supports necessary action, and faith that what needs to be done can be done.

These couples have told me what they see as their support systems. What is most important to them in a time of trouble or crisis is their family: spouse, children, parents, and in-laws. I was somewhat surprised to see the emphasis put on children. Are children, even small ones, a source of support in troublesome times? They certainly are in these families. In-laws are sometimes stereotyped as being problems, but this was not the case for these people.

Neighbors were not rated high as a source of support, which is a change from the time when our parents, and certainly our grandparents, lived. In those times life was more personal, and neighbors apparently had a greater feeling of responsibility for one another. As I stated before, I do not think this is impossible today, but it takes a concerted effort on the part of a few people to bring it about in any one neighborhood. Friends, on the other hand, were rated quite high as a source of help. Members of the clergy, services of the church, personal religious faith, prayer, and reading books all had high ratings.

In one case, a woman felt her minister and church did not help her as they might have at the time of the death of her husband. "They didn't seem to reach out to me, when I couldn't reach out for them," she said. This is unfortunate, because a congregation of a church and its ministry have a unique and necessary opportunity to "reach out" at a time such as a death in a family, and many of them do. Studies show that the potential is there, but often the performance does not come up to the potential. This discrepancy is a matter to which every church should give careful attention.

Kelley M. L. Brigman investigated the influence of religion on family strengths by asking for information from 108 family life professionals practicing in the United States. Among his conclusions are these:

> The leading category of responses concerning what dimensions of religion might be helpful to families was basic religious beliefs such as faith, hope, love, forgiveness, grace, reconciliation, the parenthood of God, and the divine worth of the individual. The second highest category was the basic religious lifestyle of commitment, responsibility, giving, sharing, and caring for others. . . Other dimensions of religion that might be helpful to families included shared beliefs, values, and family religious observances, shared religious activities, and reverence for marriage and family as a sacred lifestyle.[2]

Religious faith plays an important role in helping people meet crises as a result of some of the conclusions in Brigman's study. There is within religious faith a "therapy of hope" that keeps people positive and optimistic even in the face of what seems to be tragic circumstances. The couples in my study never succumbed to depression and hopelessness. Some sort of meaning and challenge existed in every crisis. This led to solutions to problems, strengthening of character, a greater capacity to meet further problems, and a more vital marriage relationship.

Some might argue that this religious faith as a resource for meeting crises is available to all whether they be in a church or not. To such people who think this way I would ask: "How long would the torch of religious faith keep burning apart from a community of faith that kept refueling it? How can this torch be passed adequately from one generation to another apart from a body of people to assist this continuity? How could we educate our children in any faith apart from an institution that considers teaching an important part of its life? How could we support one another through love and compassion in times of need if we did not gather for the purpose of doing this?" All good causes need to be institutionalized in one form or another. Could we educate our children apart from schools, colleges, and universities? The church gathers to worship, to learn, and to have fellowship. It scatters to bring love, reconciliation, and healing to all parts of the community. In corporate worship we experience the love of God in a way that helps us love our neighbor as ourselves. The community of faith supports us in our efforts to live our lives in our families, in our neighborhoods, and in the world to which we have been called to serve.

Couples at the beginning of their married life together need to realize that they cannot survive in this day and age without help — lots of help. Remember to keep intact that body of people closest to you — your family and your friends. Create a neighborhood of care and concern wherever you live. Become a part of some community of faith, for you will find there not only a source of power and strength but an opportunity to help others in their time of need.

Crises will come to all families in the course of time. Accept it as a part of life's adventure, which involves risks and daring, but offers great rewards to the faithful. I am constantly amazed at the coping power some people possess, particularly the couples in my longitudinal study. I was asking Erdys and Ernie to tell me how they met the crises in their lives. Erdys replied, "You know, I don't believe we have had any crises in our lives." I was somewhat startled by this remark. "But I happen to know that Ernie had a triple bypass operation several months ago," I said. "Yes, that is true," she replied, "but we didn't consider that a crisis." Ernie added that his two heart attacks were not deemed crises. Erdys said, "Yes, we have had accidents and heart attacks but did not consider them crises. In all cases, we got along well, were helped by each other and by friends. I have macular degeneration in my eyes, but my husband reads to me and I use the talking book program." By this time, I was overwhelmed by what I was hearing. Never had I seen such an expression of courage and strength of character. It seemed that they could not entertain any negative thoughts or attitudes about the events of their lives. However, I knew that they had developed over the years, beginning early in their marriage, an adequate support system consisting of family, friends, church, and religious faith — all of which transformed their life circumstances into positive experiences. Now that they are in their later years, they do not fear. What might be a dreaded crisis for some, to them is a part of life's adventure with God and friends at their side.

How will you prepare for the future, wondering what will come your way? Will there be accidents, illnesses, changes in job locations, unexpected happenings, deaths of family members and friends? Yes, they will come in some form and in some measure. And when they do, if you are prepared, you will meet them with a faith, courage, and hope you did not know you had. And I hope you can say for yourself what Albert Camus once said, "In the midst of winter, I finally learned that there was in me an invincible summer." So, marriage in the springtime can be a time of preparation that will eventually transform every winter into an "invincible summer."

Suggested Activity for Chapter 16

1. Use the following to help you consider and evaluate sources of help
   that you use or are available to you. What crises have you experienced,
   and how have you used your resources to meet them?
   Check the following as being: √√√ - always very helpful;
   √√ - helpful most of the time; √ - helpful on rare occasions;
   0 - not helpful at all.

____spouse   ____psychotherapists   ____prayer

____children   ____family doctor   ____Bible reading

____parents   ____family lawyer   ____discussion groups

____sister or brother   ____social worker   ____radio programs

____in-laws   ____minister   ____television programs

____close friends   ____church worship service   ____personal religious faith

____business associates   ____reading books   ____(other)

____neighbors   ____church school

2. What has happened in your life so far that you would describe as
   crises, as events that required an unusual amount of coping power
   and adjustment? Make a list. Write a brief statement about one
   particular crisis. What, more than any other resource, helped you
   meet this crisis? Share your insights with your partner.

CHAPTER *17*

First the Seed, Then the Plant, Then the Flower, Then the Fruit

Throughout this book, when speaking of marriage, I have often used the analogy of a growing plant. The process of growth of a plant is important to consider. The soil is prepared, the seed is planted, a tender green shoot appears and begins to grow, one looks for the flower and finally the fruit. The plant is very fragile at the beginning and needs tender, loving care. What, more than anything else, will defeat its development? Neglect! Fail to water, nourish, and cultivate, and the plant will wilt and die. It also must be protected from outside forces that would destroy it: excessive heat, bugs, wind, and weather. As it grows, it will go through various stages of change, and its needs will vary as time goes on.

Marriage is very much like a growing plant. Every year brings a new set of circumstances to it that must be negotiated. It must be carefully and lovingly nourished all the way. Neglect will cause it to die. A woman said to me, "My husband just doesn't seem to care anymore. I remember how thoughtful and attentive he was before we were married. He even opened the car door for me. He certainly doesn't do that now! I just need to feel he still appreciates me." Is this the beginning of a deterioration in a marriage? It could be.

There are many outside forces that hurt a marriage. There are many distractions that fragment the family. The daily routine brings with it the wear and tear that threatens to unravel the marital tie. If both spouses work, demands on time and energy are heightened. Stress seems to be the culprit in many contemporary marriages. We human beings tend to become computers programmed to do our work automatically and mechanically. However, computers can't love and are not lovable.

It is not easy to grow under these circumstances, yet many couples do manage. So much depends on the start they get in the early years of their married life. The romantic notion that one gets married and lives happily ever after is woefully lacking in helping a couple make progress in their relationship. It takes knowledge, awareness, a dedication to the task, and an abundance of love. Couples who have embraced these characteristics have helped me understand what it takes and how it is done. They tell me that they plan for growth. Growth is not accidental but moves toward carefully selected goals with certain skills developed along the way.

When you marry, you must realize that you will face many changes as you go along. You will change. Your spouse will change. Life all around you will change. Much will depend on how you meet these changes. Pat and Joe married while both were still in college. Joe dropped out and took the first job he could get, having lost interest in education. Pat graduated and went on for her master's degree. They grew further and further apart. After a while they found they had little in common. Joe made no effort to meet the changes that had come into Pat's life. Eventually they divorced. It is possible for a couple to meet the changes that come to them in a positive and productive manner. Joe and Pat did not do this.

Positive change is directed growth, i.e., growth that has meaning and purpose. We had a tomato plant that grew to enormous proportions, yet it only produced five tomatoes. We either had the wrong kind of seed for our desert climate or we planted it at the wrong time. Thus its growth was misdirected.

Bryant and Lucy were two exceptionally intelligent college students with whom I had the privilege of working some years ago. They excelled in many ways: academically, socially, and spiritually. Each was a campus leader and active in programs of their campus church. They sang in the choir together and shared many common interests and beliefs. When they married, all their friends predicted an ideal marriage and many happy years of married life. I saw them periodically through the early years of their life together and then lost track of them for a while. Then, word came to me that Bryant and Lucy had obtained a divorce. I was shocked and unable to believe it was true. Sometime later, I had a visit with Bryant. What had happened to a marriage that seemed so promising? This question will never be answered completely, but it seems that after five years of married life had passed, Bryant became wedded to his work. He was away from Lucy and their children more and more. His travels took him far from home and for long periods of time. Lucy complained, but to no avail. Separation led to neglect, and neglect to erosion. Bryant and Lucy became strangers. Intimacy and love disappeared. Both had grown, but not together. Both had changed, but not in the same direction. I felt saddened by this turn of events. I still return now and then to thoughts of this couple as I knew them in their early years and ask, "Did this have to happen?"

In order to understand more fully how couples meet change in their developmental process, let us turn to some of them in my study and see what they have to say.

Ruth and Jerry have been married 36 years, and their seven children have all left home. Ruth speaks about their life together at the present time: "I have started to do more things in which I am interested. This is due, in part, to the children being grown. I like books and libraries; Jerry likes plants and trees. We have learned from each other, but I feel we continue to give each other space. We are both content together and apart. I think we both find we can enjoy ourselves alone with our various hobbies much more than when we were first married. We have always been able to talk about changes in our life. Neither one of us likes things to stay the same, and so we are looking for new adventures at all times. We handle change well."

Apparently in their early years of married life, they were more demanding, more conscious of what the other was supposed to be and do. Now they are more confident, trusting, and relaxed. Many good years of relating have brought this about.

Jerry feels that while the children were still at home, he and Ruth "developed mutual perspectives toward desired goals for their future life after the children had left home." Ruth would be able to return to work in a vocation she dearly loved — being a librarian. Jerry adds, "We gave each other room to grow in different ways. I feel I have become less selfish, more responsible in my role to meet our needs, and more complete as an individual."

John and Vivienne, married 27 years, stress two important factors in their interpersonal development: an increasing ability to communicate and the wisdom to encourage each other to develop new interests and activities. Vivienne explains, "I feel that our communication skills have increased; this has occurred particularly in the development of nonverbal communication. When we have had things happen in our family which created changes, we have talked them over and decided what was best to do. We have learned to make decisions together. We have given each other the freedom to develop some activities that we do not do together. Some of these take quite a bit of time on our own (though not necessarily far apart), such as John's ham radio. We don't feel that we have to be all that interested in every project the other one does. But we are willing to listen to each other tell about his or her own interests. Altogether, there has been an increase in caring and sharing with each other."

John agrees, "We have developed very good nonverbal communication skills between us, and we have evolved a compatible and harmonious consensus on the roles each of us plays in the marriage. There are many things we enjoy doing together, such as traveling; going to concerts, plays, and athletic events; reading; dining out; and raising our children. Through the years we have developed additional common interests that we didn't have when we were first married. At the same time each of us has developed some interests in which the other doesn't participate. I spend many hours with our home computer and ham radio. Vivienne has become interested in learning other languages, needlepoint, and taking evening classes in anthropology. I think it is healthy for each to have some interests in which the other does not engage — as long as we are supportive of each other. And we are."

Hal and Bobbie, married 36 years, admit they had some difficult times in the early years of their marriage but worked through them and became stronger as a result. Bobbie states, "I have grown up and learned to appreciate our differences. As I have read, the very attributes which attract before marriage can become irritants during marriage. This happened in our marriage. I tend to be outgoing and gregarious. Hal is more quiet and introverted. After some rocky mid-years, I now appreciate his qualities again and find some formerly irritating habits endearing. We have mellowed with age and experience. Each has learned to consider where the other is coming from, so we are better able to move in the same direction." Hal adds, "We have learned to respect the other's viewpoint, which may be different from one's own. We have developed tolerance, the ability to accept criticism, and a sense of humor. We support each other."

I could add many more testimonies as to how these couples in my study grew through change, but instead I will attempt to summarize what most of them are saying.

1. All attempted to improve their ability to communicate in order to understand what was happening in each other's lives. This also helped them make decisions that were mutually agreeable and man-

age conflicts that otherwise might have become destructive.

2. The good qualities seem to have "rubbed off" on each other; so in some respects, they became more alike.

3. Tolerance and "mellowing" were noted as characteristics aiding harmony and growth.

4. Each encouraged the other to develop a healthy state of independence in order to achieve personal fulfillment.

5. Where there were differences in personality or personal preferences, there developed a spirit of acceptance and appreciation.

6. Love, caring, and unselfishness were characteristics that were quite helpful in all cases.

7. Undergirding all of the above was a commitment to work to make the marriage grow and succeed.

Couples who are in the early years of marriage need to learn from couples who have been married a number of years and who have grown into a state of greater happiness and fulfillment. The important questions to ask are "are we growing in positive directions in our marriage? What do we need to do to nourish and enrich our marriage? What resources can we find to help us?" It is my opinion that every couple within the first three years of their married life should participate in a marriage enrichment experience. Many churches provide such an opportunity. A national organization known as the Association of Couples for Marriage Enrichment will furnish information about this experience.[1] Couples under the direction of a "lead couple" trained to conduct a marriage enrichment weekend will have a growth experience that will enrich their marriages and help them learn how they can grow and develop in the future. Janet and I have conducted a number of these weekends. Comments of evaluation of the weekend from spouses were as follows:

"I learned how we can make a good marriage better."

"I know much more about myself and my spouse."

"We learned useful approaches to resolving conflict and anger."

"We know now that if a marriage is to survive, it must grow."

"To grow, a marriage must have both partners' energy and involvement."

"Most marriages have the same problems."

"I must develop my potential and keep our marriage growing."

"We know more now about how to be open with each other."

"We learned about the importance of communication."

"I liked writing what I liked about my spouse, and learning what he liked about me."

"The most helpful part to us was working on our marriage potential and contract."

"I am now motivated to work harder to make marriage and life more meaningful."

I have yet to participate in a marriage enrichment weekend in which there was anyone coming out of it not feeling inspired and motivated to make his or her marriage grow into a fuller and richer relationship. Every married couple needs to enjoy such a milestone in their lives. The first seven years of married life are the crucial ones, and many think the third year is the pivotal one. Wouldn't it be a good idea to attend a marriage enrichment weekend or encounter group during these formative years?

We often close our marriage enrichment program by having each couple work on their "Marriage Potential and Contract." Couples seem to feel this insures the value of the weekend to be a lasting experience in the months to come. Following the work on this instrument, we join together in a "Service of Agape," which concludes by having each couple repeat their wedding vows.

David Mace, in an article in the publication *Marriage Encounter*, writes:

> In recent years, my work in the field of marriage enrichment has brought me into close touch with thousands of couples. I have seen some remarkable evidences of growth and change. I believe that most married people, if they only know it, are sitting on a gold mine. There are tremendous possibilities, unclaimed and unappropriated, in every couple relationship. We have the raw materials. But we have to meet the challenge and pay the price, if we really mean to build a truly happy, healthy marriage.[2]

This chapter began with the use of a growing plant as an analogy for a growing marriage. We give it tender, loving care from seed to plant to flower to fruit. Each phase in the life cycle of the plant must be understood, cultivated, and nourished. The same is true of the center of all life — marriage and the family. Each one of us needs to be committed to the kind of growth that will produce a healthier world in which we can live and nurture our children. Such commitment "meet[s] the challenge and pay[s] the price," but the rewards are great and unending.

In 1 Corinthians 13, Paul admonishes us to grow. In my translation of verse 11 I believe I have been faithful to its true meaning.

"When I was a child, I said childish things, my ideas were not fully developed, and I often acted immaturely, but when, over the years,

I grew and developed, I gave up my childish ways, and lived and loved as an adult."

Sometimes when I look back on the time my partner and I were first married, it seems that we were mere children entering a big world about which we knew so little. And we must have done many childish things, as most couples do, in those early years. As time went by, however, unceasing effort, careful planning, enduring love, and the grace of God helped us grow and develop, give up childish ways, and now live and love as adults. This has been the experience of almost all the couples with whom I have worked, who now have happy and healthy marriages. This is the possibility for all of you who come along the way.

Suggested Activity for Chapter 17

1. Create a plan for personal growth. List two or three personal characteristics in which you would like to improve. Identify your potential for growth in each one of these. Where would you like to be a year from now? What concrete things can you do to get there?
2. Create a plan for relational growth. List some areas in your relationship with your partner in which you would like improvement. What changes would you like to make over the next year? Commit yourselves to work together to make it happen.
3. In 1 Corinthians 13:11, Paul indicates the need to grow from immaturity to maturity. What are some of the childish ways couples use in attempting to meet their differences? What are the qualities of a mature person and how do these help in a marital relationship?

Epilogue

The title of this book is *The Springtime of Love and Marriage*. It is my hope that couples who are just beginning their journey of life together could benefit from couples who have gone on ahead and successfully negotiated the turns, bumps, detours, rest stops, weariness of the long hours, heat of the desert, exhilaration of climbing mountains, and beauty of the wilderness and coastal plains of married life.

An old friend of mine, whom I consider to be very wise, once said, "If you want to know how to get to a certain destination, ask someone who has made the journey before you." The couples in these happy, healthy marriages have arrived or are well on their way. They should give all of us who are coming along courage, inspiration, and faith for our marital adventure. Perhaps all of us who are touched by their lives and experiences could join together in the words of the writer to the Hebrews:

"Therefore, since we are surrounded by so great a cloud of witnesses, let us also lay aside every weight, and sin which clings so closely, and let us run with perseverance the race that is set before us, looking to Jesus the pioneer and perfecter of our faith . . ." (Hebrews 12:1, 2a).

Notes

Chapter 1

[1] Stella Chess, Alexander Thomas, and Herbert G. Birch, *Your Child Is a Person* (New York: The Viking Press, 1965); and Alexander Thomas and Stella Chess, *Temperament and Development* (New York: Brunner/Mazel, Inc., 1977).

Chapter 2

[1] Larry L. Bumpass and James A. Sweet, "Differences in Marital Instability, 1970," *American Sociological Review*, 37 (1972), pp. 754-766.

[2] Lloyd Saxton, *The Individual, Marriage and the Family* (Belmont, CA: Wadsworth Publishing Co., 1977).

Chapter 3

[1] Eleanor D. Macklin, "Heterosexual Cohabitation Among Unmarried University Students," *The Family Coordinator* (October, 1972), pp. 463-472.

[2] Robert O. Blood, *The Family* (New York: The Free Press, 1972), p. 340.

[3] James R. Hine, *Grounds for Marriage* (Danville, Ill.: The Interstate Printers and Publishers, 1977), p. v.

[4] One recommended text is Lawrence Crawley, James Malfetti, Ernest Stewart, and Nina Dias, *Reproduction, Sex, and Preparation for Marriage* (Englewood Cliffs, NJ: Prentice-Hall, Inc., 1973).

Chapter 4

[1] James R. Hine, *What Comes After You Say, "I Love You"?* (Palo Alto, CA: Pacific Books, Publishers, 1980).

Chapter 5

[1] E. Walster, V. Aronson, D. Abraham, and L. Rottman, "Importance of Physical Attractiveness in Dating Behavior," *Journal of Personality and Social Psychology,* (1966), pp. 508-516.

[2] John Money, *Love and Love Sickness: The Science of Sex; Gender Difference and Pair Bonding* (Baltimore: The John Hopkins University Press, 1980).

[3] Rollo May, *Love and Will* (New York: Dell Publishing Co., Inc., 1969).

[4] Zick Rubin, *Liking and Loving* (New York: Holt, Rinehart and Winston, Inc., 1973).

[5] James R. Hine, *What Comes After You Say, "I Love You"?* (Palo Alto, CA: Pacific Books Publishers, 1980), pp. 30-34.

Chapter 6

[1] Jerry Sonenblick and Martha Sowerwine, *The Legality of Love* (New York: Jove Publications, 1981), p. 99.

[2] Clifford J. Sager, *Marriage Contracts and Couple Therapy* (New York: Brunner/ Mazel, Publishers, 1976), pp. 10, 11.

[3] Natalia Belting and James R. Hine, *Your Wedding Workbook* (Danville, IL: The Interstate Printers and Publishers, 1977).

Chapter 7

[1] Mordecai L. Brill, Marlene Halpin, and William H. Genné, *Write Your Own Wedding* (New York: Association Press, 1973).

[2] Natalia Belting and James R. Hine, *Your Wedding Workbook* (Danville, IL: The Interstate Printers and Publishers, 1977).

Chapter 8

[1] Salvador Minuchin and H. Charles Fishman, *Family Therapy Techniques* (Cambridge, MA: Harvard University Press, 1981), p. 198.

[2] Conrad Weiser, *Dancing All the Dances, Singing All the Songs* (Philadelphia: The Fortress Press, 1975), p. 40.

[3] *Gallup Opinion Index*, Report No. 112, October 1974, pp. 9-13.

[4] U. S. National Center for Health Statistics, 1973.

Chapter 9

[1] The Role Concept Comparison Inventory is adapted from the one in *Your Marriage: Analysis and Renewal* by James R. Hine (Danville, IL: The Interstate Printers and Publishers, 1976), p. 19.

Chapter 10

[1] Helmut Thielicke, *The Ethics of Sex* (New York: Harper and Row, Publishers, Inc., 1964), pp. 66-69.

[2] See James R. Hine, *What Comes After You Say, "I Love You"?* (Palo Alto, CA: Pacific Books Publishers, 1980), p. 208.

[3] Annette G. Godow, *Human Sexuality* (St. Louis: The C. V. Mosby Co., 1982), pp. 362-365.

[4] William H. Masters and Virginia E. Johnson, *Human Sexual Response* (Boston: Little, Brown and Company, 1966).

[5] Hine, *op.cit.*, pp. 214-215.

Chapter 11

[1] Helmut Thielicke, *The Ethics of Sex* (New York: Harper and Row, Publishers, Inc., 1964), p. 8.

Chapter 12

[1] Ashley Montagu, *Touching: The Human Significance of the Skin* (New York: Columbia University Press, 1971), pp. 261, 262.

Chapter 13

[1] George R. Bach and Peter Wyden, *The Intimate Enemy: How to Fight Fair in Love and Marriage* (New York: William Morrow and Company, 1969).

[2] Carl A. Ridley, Arthur W. Avery, Jan F. Harrell, Leslie A. Leigh, and Judy Dent, *Conflict Management: A Premarital Training Program in Mutual Problem Solving.* This pamphlet is available from Division of Child Development and Family Relations, University of Arizona, Tucson, AZ 85721.

[3] James R. Hine, *What Comes After You Say, "I Love You"?* (Palo Alto, CA: Pacific Books Publishers, 1980), pp. 190, 191.

[4] David Mace, *Love and Anger in Marriage* (Grand Rapids: Zondervan Publishing House, 1982).

[5] Harry Stack Sullivan, *Conceptions of Modern Psychiatry* (New York: W.W. Norton and Co., 1946), pp. 42, 43.

Chapter 14

[1] E. G. Williamson, "The Meaning of Communication in Counseling," *Personnel and Guidance Journal*, 38 (1959), pp. 6-14.

[2] Sidney B. Simon, Leland W. Howe, and Howard Kirschenbaum, *Values Clarification* (New York: Hart Publishing Co., Inc., 1972), p. 13.

[3] See Gerhard Lenski, *The Religious Factor* (New York: Doubleday and Co., 1961).

Chapter 15

[1] Rudolf Dreikurs, *The Challenge of Marriage* (New York: Duell, Sloan and Pearce, 1946), p. 204.

[2] E. E. LeMasters, "Parenthood as Crisis," *Journal of Marriage and Family Living*, vol. 19, no. 4 (1957), pp. 352-355.

[3] Alicerose Barman, *Your First Months with Your Baby*, Public Affairs Pamphlet No. 478, 1972, p. 21.

Chapter 16

[1] John Donne, "Devotions," VI.

[2] Kelley M. L. Brigman, "Religion and Family Strengths: An Approach to Wellness," *Wellness Perspectives*, vol. 1, no. 2 (Spring, 1984).

Chapter 17

[1] The address of the Association of Couples for Marriage Enrichment is 459 S. Church Street, Winston-Salem, NC 27108.

[2] David R. Mace, "Building a Marriage," *Marriage Encounter*, August, 1982, pp. 10, 11.